MERCHANT GOURMET — LIMITED EDITION — ...AGNE LENTILS — Simply Cooked

MERCHANT GOURMET — NEW — Zingy KOREAN-STYLE — Simply Cooked — Grains

MERCHANT GOURMET — PUY LENTILS — Simply Cooked

MERCHANT GOURMET — BELUGA LENTILS — Simply Cooked

MERCHANT GOURMET — SUPER SEEDS — with Quinoa & Chia

MERCHANT GOURMET — Smoky SPANISH-STYLE — Grains & Rice

MERCHANT GOURMET — FREEKEH — Simply Cooked

MER... GOUR... — QUINOA — Red & White — Simply Cooked

...NT GOURMET — NEW — Zingy KOREAN-STYLE — Grains

MER GO — PUY — Sim...

UNLOCK THE WORLD'S LARDER

...RCHANT GOURMET — ...Y LENTILS — Simply Cooked

MERCHANT GOURMET — QUINOA — Red & White — Simply Cooked

MERCHANT GOURMET — NEW — Pesto-ey ITALIAN-INFUSED — Grains

MERCHANT GOURMET — FREEKEH — Simply Cooked

MERCHANT GOURMET — NEW — PUGLIA LENTILS — with Truffle Infused Oil

...RCHANT GOURMET — ...A LENTILS — ...ruffle Infused Oil

MERCHANT GOURMET — NEW — Zingy KOREAN-STYLE — Grains

MERCHANT GOURMET — PUY LENTILS — Simply Cooked

MERCHANT GOURMET — Smoky SPANISH-STYLE — Grains & Rice

MERCHANT GOURMET — SUPER SEEDS — with Quinoa & Chia — Simply Cooked

MERCHANT GOURMET — BELUGA LENTILS — Simply Cooked

MER GO — Z... KOREA...

MERCHANT GOURMET — FREEKEH — Simply Cooked

MERCHANT GOURMET — NEW — Pesto-ey ITALIAN-INFUSED — Grains

MERCHANT GOURMET — PUY LENTILS — Simply Cooked

MERCHANT
GOURMET

The Pulses & Grains Cookbook

Delicious recipes for every day,
with lentils, grains, seeds and chestnuts

Recipes by Becks Wilkinson
Photography by Kim Lightbody

Hardie Grant

QUADRILLE

CONTENTS

A BIT ABOUT MERCHANT GOURMET

At Merchant Gourmet, we love to give fresh inspiration to anyone who enjoys good food and shares our zest for discovering new ingredients. As the UK's Number One pulses, grains and chestnut brand, we're on a mission to introduce as many people as possible to these amazing ingredients and to help everyone make them a part of their cooking repertoire, every day.

Merchant Gourmet was founded in 1995 by brothers Mark and Oliver Leatham, who had a passion for exploring real food. Ever since then, our dedicated team has been out sourcing the finest ingredients from across the world. We were the first brand to bring speciality foods like Camargue red rice and ready-to-eat chestnuts to the UK market. Then we took things a step further, launching our ready-to-eat Puy lentil and quinoa pouches – the first of their kind in the country. Ready in a flash, they made convenience food healthy and, as a result, grains and pulses really took off.

Today our range offers a growing variety of products that go from pouch to plate in under one minute! Consisting of lentils, quinoa, wholegrains and seeds, our ready-to-eat pouches offer a nutritious alternative to white rice, pasta and potatoes; some pouches have been simply cooked with a dash of water and a drizzle of olive oil and others have been infused with globally inspired flavours – ideal for when you're short on time but you don't want to compromise on health or flavour. We also have a great range of dried pulses and grains for when you have a little more time on your hands!

We believe in living and eating well even when you're in a hurry, and that's why we've written this book. In these pages you'll find the most inspiring, accessible and creative recipes – from lentil breakfast pancakes and freekeh porridge with poached pears, to stuffed, roasted red peppers, quinoa-crusted chicken and incredible lemon cheesecake with a mixed seed base.

We hope you love these recipes as much as we do; we think you'll be amazed at how versatile and delicious these lentils, grains, seeds and chestnuts can be!

OUR INGREDIENTS

PUY LENTILS

Puy lentils come from the region of Le Puy-en-Velay in southern France. The area is formed from ancient volcanic lava domes. Combined with the high altitude of the valley, this creates the perfect conditions to grow the delicate Puy lentil. Due to these unique growing conditions, the lentil has its own protected designation of origin status – which means that, to use the name 'Puy lentil', the product must be grown without any pesticides or irrigation and harvested and packed in the region of Puy.

The Puy cooperative
The Puy region has a 50km perimeter, and is home to 88 small villages, within which there are around 600 farmers. At Merchant Gourmet, Puy lentils are sourced from a cooperative of farmers within the region. They get paid upfront by the lentil suppliers and offered subsidized insurance to help support their business, particularly during bad harvests, as Puy crops are so fragile and dependent on the climate due to their strict growing conditions.

A bit about texture
What makes Puy lentils so special is their delicate thin membrane, caused by the special growing conditions. This means the lentils are incredibly delicate, yet retain a firm bite, don't lose their texture and cook faster than other lentils.

BELUGA® LENTILS

Beluga® is a type of small, black lentil which gets its name from the resemblance to beluga caviar. The lentils are grown in the cool, dry climates of Canada and America's northern plains and are less common than red, yellow and green lentils. Unlike red and yellow lentils, black Beluga® lentils retain their shape and al-dente texture when cooked. They have a delicate taste and are fantastic at absorbing other flavours.

Why Beluga® lentils are good for you
Beluga® lentils are high in protein and dietary fibre and are a rich source of iron. Black lentils, such as Beluga®, provide certain phytochemicals, including anthocyanins – powerful antioxidants also found in dark berries like blueberries and blackberries.

CHAMPAGNE LENTILS

Champagne lentils are grown in the heart of the Champagne region of France, famous for its celebrated sparkling wines and high quality of soil. They are slightly rose-coloured and thinner than regular lentils, with a subtle, nutty taste. Champagne lentils can be used just like any other lentil in a variety of dishes and they make a great alternative to meat.

A bit of history
Lentils are among the most ancient of vegetables. The 'lentillon de Champagne' is one of the older varieties and has been harvested since Roman times. A similar variety was found in an Egyptian tomb, examples of which are kept in the Louvre. The pink lentils are a rare commodity, with an annual production of approximately 100 tonnes. It's the unique soil composition of the Champagne region that gives the lentil its sweet delicate flavour.

Why Champagne lentils are good for you
The nutritional value of Champagne lentils is extensive. High in fibre and protein, the lentils release their energy more slowly, which can help you feel fuller for longer.

QUINOA

Quinoa is a tiny, bead-shaped seed with a wonderfully nutty flavour. Commonly regarded as a grain in the UK, quinoa comes in three colours – red, white and black. It is primarily grown in Peru, Bolivia and Ecuador (where it used to be the go-to grain for sustaining workers), but we're now lucky enough to have it growing on our doorstep in the UK, too. Once cooked, the quinoa grains quadruple in size and become almost translucent. Quinoa's texture and flavour are delicious when mixed with all sorts of other ingredients.

Why quinoa is good for you
Quinoa is just what you need as part of a healthy and balanced diet: described as the 'perfect protein', it has a low glycaemic index to help control your blood sugar levels and provides a great source of fibre, which helps to keep your digestive system happy.

FREEKEH

Freekeh – sometimes referred to as 'frikeh' or 'farik' in Arabic (meaning 'rubbed') – is a traditional Middle Eastern grain. It's harvested young whilst the wheat is still green and the seeds are soft. It's then toasted, dried and rubbed to give it its characteristic texture, colour and deep, smoky flavour. It's perfect for giving an extra bite to your salads and an extra dimension to stir-fries and soups.

A bit of history
Freekeh production dates back to 2300BC, when an eastern Mediterranean nation was anticipating an attack on their city. Because they were worried about losing their crops and starving, they picked the early green heads of wheat and stored them. When the city came under fire, the green wheat was burnt. However, the people discovered that, when rubbed, the grains were still edible.

Why freekeh is good for you
Freekeh is considered a 'supergrain' by some. It's a good source of fibre and a more nutritious alternative to couscous or white rice, containing many of the same nutrients as farro and quinoa.

WHEATBERRIES

Wheatberries are – quite literally – the berries from wheat plants. These golden-coloured grains are whole, largely unprocessed (apart from a cleaning stage that removes inpurities) wheat kernels which contain all three parts of the grain, but with the inedible, outermost hull removed. They are the least processed form of wheat and come in lots of different varieties: hard or soft, winter or spring, and red or white.

Let's talk about taste!
They have a sweet, creamy yet nutty flavour that works just as well in savoury meat and vegetable dishes as they do in sweeter puddings and breakfast recipes. The berries hold their shape and keep their chewy bite long after cooking, which makes them perfect in winter soups.

WHOLEWHEAT GIANT COUSCOUS

Giant couscous is, in fact, not really couscous at all. It is the name given to tiny balls of pasta usually made from wheat flour, and toasted. It has a bouncy texture and is a brilliant go-to ingredient for wholesome salads.

A bit of history

Giant couscous came about in the 1950s after Israel's first president, David Ben-Gurion, asked the Osem Food Company to develop a wheat-based substitute for rice during the country's austerity period. Popular in Jordan, Syria and Lebanon, it is also known as Israeli couscous, North African berkukes or Palestinian maftoul. Its name depends on the type of flour it is made from, or the country it is from. It can also be called ptitim, maftouc, mograbiah, gredola, Jersualem couscous or Ben-Gurion rice.

Let's talk about taste!

Giant couscous is twice as big as the more common small, yellow, semolina-based couscous from North Africa. It is toasted rather than dried, which gives it a nutty flavour and it feels light but hearty. Like pasta, it has a chewy bite, can stand up to a good sauce and is great mixed into salads. It goes perfectly with Middle Eastern dishes like tagines.

WHITE QUINOA

PUY LENTILS

CHAMPAGNE LENTILS

CHESTNUTS

RED QUINOA

CHESTNUTS

Sweet chestnuts, not to be confused with poisonous horse chestnuts, are the edible nuts of the *Castanea sativa* tree. These trees have been cultivated for over 2,000 years, providing a staple food over the centuries. Chestnuts are traditionally roasted in their outer brown husks and then peeled before eating. They have a sweet flavour and floury texture and are delicious when eaten whole as a snack, or in both sweet and savoury dishes.

A bit of history
The sweet chestnut tree is native to southern Europe and what is now Turkey, but has now been widely cultivated around the world. The hardiness of the sweet chestnut tree is evident from the many ancient trees across Europe – the oldest being the Hundred Horse Chestnut Tree near Mount Etna in Sicily.

Why chestnuts are good for you
Chestnuts contain low levels of fat and calories in comparison to other nuts. They are rich in starchy carbs and fibre, and are a good source of vitamin C and vitamin B_6.

FREEKEH

WHOLEWHEAT GIANT COUSCOUS

BELUGA LENTILS

WHEATBERRIES

AMARANTH

Amaranth is an ancient, nutrient-packed grain that has been cultivated for 8,000 years and which originated in the Americas. It can be bought as grains, popped or puffed, or ground into a flour. The grains come from the plant of the same name, *Amaranthus*. Its flowers are densely packed with seeds, with each one producing as many as 60,000.

Let's talk about taste!
Neither sweet nor savoury, amaranth has a subtle, slightly peppery flavour. When cooked, it looks a bit like brown caviar. Try it cooked as porridge or mixed with other grains in salads. When popped it takes on a nuttier flavour and a crunchy texture.

Why amaranth is good for you
The amaranth plant is a relative of beetroot, spinach and Swiss chard, which means it shares many of their nutritional benefits. It is packed with goodness, contains three times more fibre than wheat does, and is gluten free.

CHIA SEEDS

Chia seeds are small, oval and nutrient-packed. They can be eaten raw or soaked, which makes them swell and become gelatinous. Chia is a species of plant in the mint family. Like amaranth, its seeds are thought to have first been cultivated by the Aztecs in Mexico. Its name comes from the Mexican word 'chian', meaning oily.

A bit about flavour and texture
Chia seeds are mottled brown, grey, white or black. They can be sprinkled raw over salads or added to smoothies, porridge, yoghurt and other foods. When soaked, they can be added to juices and cold drinks, or mixed with liquids to make a pudding. The seeds are flavourless, so they can be added to recipes without affecting the taste.

Heating the seeds doesn't have any negative effect on the nutrients, which makes them great for use in bread and bakery products.

And did you know?
Soaked chia seeds act as a brilliant egg alternative in vegan baking.
1 tsp ground chia + 3 tbsp water = 1 egg

Why chia seeds are good for you
Chia seeds are rich in plant omega-3 fatty acids. They have a similar nutrient profile to flax and sesame seeds.

SUNFLOWER SEEDS

These seeds come from – of course – sunflowers! The flower produces these small seeds that are greyish in colour and that come in dark shells called husks.

Why sunflower seeds are good for you
Sunflower seeds are packed full of key nutrients including vitamin E, vitamin B_1, magnesium, protein and fibre!

What do they taste like?
They have a mild flavour with a firm texture.

PUMPKIN SEEDS

Pumpkin seeds are edible, flat, oval-shaped dark green seeds. They can be roasted to create a delicious crunchy snack.

Why pumpkin seeds are good for you
These little seeds are nutritional power-houses containing zinc, B vitamins (riboflavin, niacin), magnesium, iron and protein. They also contain high levels of a plant-based essential fatty acid that contributes to the maintenance of normal blood cholesterol levels.

Let's talk about taste!
The seeds have a chewy texture and a subtly sweet, nutty flavour.

PUMPKIN SEEDS

CHIA SEEDS

SUNFLOWER SEEDS

AMARANTH

Breakfast & Brunch

FREEKEH PORRIDGE WITH POACHED SPICED PEARS, APPLE & ALMONDS

A warming and totally satisfying breakfast that's packed full of protein and slow release energy to keep you going all morning. It will make the perfect start to a chilly morning.

 SERVES 2   25–30 MINS    VEGAN

INGREDIENTS

- 500ml apple juice
- 4 tbsp agave syrup
- 1 tsp vanilla paste or 2 tsp vanilla extract
- 3 black peppercorns
- 1 cinnamon stick
- ½ orange
- 2 Conference pears
- 1 x 250g pouch of ready cooked Freekeh
- 50g jumbo oats
- 350ml hazelnut milk
- 1 apple
- 2 tbsp dairy-free yoghurt
- 2 tbsp hazelnuts, roughly chopped

METHOD

1. Put the apple juice and agave syrup in a small, deep saucepan. Add the vanilla, peppercorns and cinnamon stick. Thickly slice the orange half and add it to the pan.

2. Peel the pears. Bring the liquid in the pan to the boil and add the pears. They should be covered with liquid so, if not, top up with a little water. Place a small saucer on top of the pears so they are immersed and cannot float to the surface and cook unevenly. Simmer over a low heat for 15–20 minutes until the pears are soft enough for the point of a knife to pierce the flesh easily.

3. While the pears are poaching, empty the pouch of cooked freekeh into another saucepan, add the oats and pour in the hazelnut milk. Bring to a slow simmer, stirring occasionally to stop the milk catching on the bottom of the pan. Add a good ladleful of the poached pear liquid to sweeten the freekeh. As nut milk often curdles when heated with another liquid, keep stirring and, when the porridge has thickened (after about 10 minutes), take it off the heat. Leave it to rest for 2 minutes so any remaining liquid is absorbed.

4. When you are ready to serve, lift out the poached pears, cut them in half lengthways and scoop out the cores. Coarsely grate the apple and divide the porridge between 2 bowls.

5. Top each bowl with a tablespoon of yoghurt, some grated apple, the pear halves and a good sprinkling of almonds.

ASPARAGUS & SUPER SEED OMELETTE WITH HERBY CRÈME FRAÎCHE

A substantial breakfast or brunch dish that's full of contrasting textures and flavours. The sharpness of the feta, the freshness of the asparagus spears and herbs, the texture of the super seeds, and the fiery chilli flakes all complement each other perfectly.

 SERVES 1–2  10 MINS   VEGETARIAN

INGREDIENTS
- 4 large free-range eggs
- 2 tbsp milk
- 25g feta
- 100g asparagus spears
- ½ x 250g pouch of ready cooked Super Seeds with Quinoa & Chia
- a handful mixed fresh herbs, such as flat-leaf parsley, tarragon, thyme
- 4 tbsp crème fraîche
- 1 tbsp butter
- pinch of dried chilli flakes
- salt and black pepper

METHOD
1. Whisk the eggs and milk together and season with salt and pepper.

2. Crumble the feta and slice the asparagus spears in half lengthways. Put the lentils in a bowl and stir to separate them.

3. Remove any tough stalks from the herbs and roughly chop the leaves. Stir the herbs into the crème fraîche.

4. Place a large frying pan over a medium heat and, when hot, add the butter. When it melts and foams, spread out the halved asparagus spears in the pan in a single layer. Cook for 2 minutes. Pour the beaten eggs into the pan and, using a spatula, gently stir the eggs through the asparagus. Scatter over most of the super seeds, reserving a few for garnish, followed by the crumbled feta. Cook until the eggs are just set.

5. Using the spatula, carefully roll the omelette out of the pan onto a plate so it folds neatly in half. Divide between 2 serving plates (if feeding 2 people) and serve with the reserved super seeds and chilli flakes scattered over. Accompany with the herby crème fraîche.

SPINACH & LENTIL PANCAKES WITH TOMATO & CORIANDER SALSA

This recipe gives a new twist to traditional pancakes and, if you have a blender, it couldn't be quicker or easier to make. The Beluga® lentils give the pancakes a warm peppery flavour, while the salsa adds freshness and colour. As well as the salsa, the pancakes would also be delicious served topped with poached eggs or natural yoghurt.

 SERVES 2–4   25 MINS  VEGETARIAN

INGREDIENTS

- 1 x 250g pouch of ready cooked Beluga® Lentils
- 100ml milk
- 2 free-range eggs
- 50g baby leaf spinach
- 100g plain flour
- 1 tsp baking powder
- ½ tsp cumin seeds
- 8 cherry tomatoes
- 15g fresh coriander
- 2 tbsp olive oil, plus a little extra for greasing
- 2 tbsp balsamic vinegar
- salt and black pepper

METHOD

1. Turn on the oven to its lowest setting so you can keep the pancakes warm as you cook them.

2. Blend half the pouch of lentils (125g) with the milk, eggs, spinach, flour, baking powder and cumin seeds until you have a thick mixture. Don't worry if it's not smooth as this will give the pancakes added texture.

3. Place a large frying pan over a medium heat and lightly oil the pan. When it is hot, add 3 or 4 large tablespoons of the pancake batter (1 tablespoon per pancake), depending on the size of the pan. Cook for 2–3 minutes until the undersides are golden, then turn the pancakes over and cook for a further 2–3 minutes until the other sides are golden. Remove from the pan and keep warm in the oven while you cook the rest of the batter. There should be enough to make 8–10 pancakes, depending on size.

4. Empty the remaining 125g lentils into a small bowl. Halve the tomatoes and lightly crush them so their juices run out. Add the halved tomatoes and their juices to the lentils. Chop the coriander and add to the bowl with the olive oil and balsamic vinegar. Season with salt and pepper.

5. Divide the little pancakes between serving plates and serve with the salsa.

TOMATOEY LENTILS, SCRAMBLED EGGS, BACON & SAUSAGE BURRITOS

Soft tortilla wraps rolled around a filling that is packed full of good things. You can vary the vegetables according to personal taste or to what you have available and substitute another hard cheese for the Cheddar we've used, if you prefer.

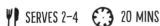 SERVES 2–4   20 MINS

INGREDIENTS
- 150g cherry tomatoes
- 1 sprig of fresh thyme
- 1 tbsp olive oil
- 4 rashers of bacon
- 4 chipolata sausages
- 4 free-range eggs
- 1 tbsp milk
- 1 x 250g pouch of ready cooked Tomatoey French Puy & Green Lentils
- 1 tbsp butter
- 4 tortilla wraps
- 25g Cheddar cheese, grated
- a handful of rocket
- salt and black pepper

METHOD

1. Preheat the oven to 190°C (170°C fan)/Gas mark 5. Halve the cherry tomatoes and spread them out on a baking tray. Pull the leaves off the thyme sprig and sprinkle over the tomato halves. Drizzle with the olive oil and season with salt and pepper. Put the bacon and sausages on another tray. Put both trays in the oven and cook for 10 minutes, or until the bacon is crisp and the sausages are cooked through.

2. Whisk the eggs and milk together in a jug.

3. Heat 2 saucepans over a medium heat. Tip the lentils into one pan, add a splash of water and leave the lentils to heat through. Melt the butter in the other pan and when it is foaming, pour in the beaten eggs. Stir the eggs slowly until they are just set.

4. Lay the wraps flat on a board and divide the lentils between them. Top with the grated cheese, scrambled eggs, bacon and sausages, finishing with the tomatoes and rocket.

5. Carefully roll up the tortillas and enjoy!

BLACKBERRY, LENTIL & ELDERFLOWER SMOOTHIE BOWL

This gorgeous smoothie is rich in natural plant-based protein so there's no need to spend money buying expensive powders any more. Don't be put off by the thought of lentils in a smoothie as the Champagne ones used here have a mild, nutty flavour that works really well with the blackberries and elderflower without overpowering them. You can mix things up by using different toppings and yoghurts, substituting dairy-free yoghurt if you prefer. As well as keeping you going through the morning, it makes a great recovery drink after a strenuous workout.

The smoothie will be thicker than a normal one, which means you can pile on lots of toppings and they won't sink. If you want a thinner shake, just increase the quantity of juice.

 SERVES 2–4   4 MINS   VEGETARIAN

INGREDIENTS

For the smoothie
- 1 x 250g pouch of ready cooked Champagne Lentils
- 1 large banana
- 250g frozen blackberries (or a mixture of different berries)
- 1 tbsp maple syrup
- 1 tbsp milled flaxseed
- 120g thick natural yoghurt (or a flavoured yoghurt of your choice)
- 100ml elderflower and apple juice

Suggested toppings
- blackberries, raspberries, blueberries
- flaxseeds, pumpkin seeds
- almonds, hazelnuts, pecans, coconut flakes
- freeze-dried berries

METHOD

1. Blend together all the smoothie ingredients until thick and the mixture has the consistency of soft ice cream.

2. Divide the mixture between serving bowls and add the toppings of your choice. Serve at once before the smoothie starts to melt!

To make this vegan: use dairy-free yoghurt.

SPICY CHORIZO, KALE & LENTIL HASH WITH SUMAC & FRIED EGGS

This brunch dish is a good way of using up those leftover cooked potatoes. Sumac is a dark red spice with a tangy, lemony flavour, often used in Middle Eastern and Mediterranean dishes. It adds both colour and flavour to the hash.

 SERVES 2    15 MINS

INGREDIENTS
- 75g chorizo, diced
- 1 small red onion
- 2 cloves of garlic
- 100g cooked potatoes, chopped
- 1 tsp smoked paprika
- a handful of kale, chopped
- 1 x 250g pouch of ready cooked Puy Lentils
- 1 tbsp olive oil
- 2 free-range eggs
- 1 tsp sumac
- salt and black pepper

METHOD

1. Place a large frying pan over a high heat, add the diced chorizo and fry briskly so it colours and releases some of the oil it contains. Lower the heat to medium and cook for a further 2 minutes.

2. Peel and cut the onion into 1cm dice and finely slice the garlic. Add them to the pan and fry for 2 minutes until softened.

3. Add the potatoes and smoked paprika and fry until the potatoes are crisp and golden, about 5 minutes. Add the kale and lentils and cook for a further 2 minutes, stirring constantly. Season with salt and pepper.

4. Heat the oil in a separate frying pan and crack in the eggs. Fry until the whites are set but the yolks are still runny.

5. Divide the hash between serving plates. Top with a fried egg and sprinkle with the sumac and some extra pepper. Serve at once.

ORANGEY QUINOA GRANOLA

Make a batch of this crunchy, nutty granola at the weekend and you'll have enough to last you all week – maybe even longer, as the granola can be stored in an airtight container for up to 2 weeks.

SERVES 6 · **35 MINS** (V) **VEGETARIAN**

INGREDIENTS

- 1 x 250g pouch of ready cooked Red & White Quinoa
- 250g jumbo rolled oats
- 150g runny honey
- finely grated zest of 1 orange
- 50g pistachios
- 50g hazelnuts
- 100g raisins
- yoghurt or milk, to serve

METHOD

1. Preheat the oven to 190°C (170°C fan)/Gas mark 5.

2. Mix together the quinoa and oats in a large bowl. Add the honey and orange zest and stir until well mixed.

3. Line a large baking tray with baking parchment and spread out the grain mixture in the tray in an even layer. Bake in the oven for about 30 minutes, stirring and turning over the mixture every 10 minutes, until it is golden and crunchy.

4. Roughly chop the pistachios and hazelnuts and mix with the raisins.

5. Transfer the toasted grain mixture to a bowl and stir in the nuts and raisins. Leave to cool and then store in an airtight container. Serve with yoghurt or milk.

To make this vegan: replace the honey with maple syrup and serve with dairy-free yoghurt or milk.

OVERNIGHT OATS WITH MANGO, MILK & HONEY

When you're pushed for time, prepare this nutritious breakfast the night before, spoon it into jars, tubs or bowls and pop it in the fridge. The next morning it's ready to eat straight away or take with you to work. It's equally good made with vegan milks and yoghurts and you can substitute other fruits if you wish.

 SERVES 2   CHILL OVERNIGHT   (V) VEGETARIAN

INGREDIENTS

- 1 x 250g pouch of ready cooked Super Seeds with Quinoa & Chia
- 100g jumbo rolled oats
- 50g raspberries
- 150g mango flesh
- 100g natural yoghurt
- 100ml milk
- 1 tbsp runny honey
- extra fruit or yoghurt, to serve (optional)

METHOD

1. Put the super seeds, oats and raspberries in a bowl.

2. Pulse the mango, yoghurt, milk and honey in a blender but don't make it too smooth as it's nice to have small pieces of mango running through it.

3. Add the blended mixture to the super seed mixture in the bowl and stir the two together until evenly mixed. Spoon into jars, tubs or bowls, cover and store in the fridge overnight.

4. Eat plain or topped with extra fruit and yoghurt.

To make this vegan: replace the honey with maple syrup and use dairy-free yoghurt and milk.

SHAKSHUKA WITH LENTILS & FETA

Shakshuka is a spicy vegetable stew from the Middle East made with red peppers, tomatoes and onions and topped with eggs. It's a vibrantly coloured dish and, as it's cooked in one pot, makes light work of the washing up. You can add different toppings depending on what you have in the fridge – we like crumbled salty feta and cooling yoghurt or labneh (an extra thick and tangy Middle Eastern yoghurt) to cut through the rich tomato sauce. We've also added lentils here for extra protein, and to keep you fuller for longer. Serve it with toasted sourdough bread to soak up all the spicy juices.

 SERVES 4   35 MINS   VEGETARIAN

INGREDIENTS

- 1 onion
- 3 cloves of garlic
- 2 tbsp olive oil
- 1 large jar of flame-roasted red peppers (280g drained weight)
- ½ tsp smoked paprika
- 2 tbsp tomato purée
- 2 tbsp harissa
- 1 x 400g can of chopped tomatoes
- 1 x 250g pouch of ready cooked Beluga® Lentils
- 4 free-range eggs
- 4 tbsp natural yoghurt or labneh
- 30g feta, crumbled
- 3 tbsp finely chopped fresh flat-leaf parsley
- salt and black pepper
- toasted sourdough bread, to serve

METHOD

1. Peel and finely slice the onion and garlic. Heat the oil in a wide, shallow pan or large frying pan over a medium heat, add the onion and garlic and fry for about 6 minutes until the onion has softened and started to caramelize.

2. Drain the peppers, reserving the liquid for the sauce. Slice the peppers into 1cm wide strips.

3. Add the paprika, tomato purée and harissa to the pan and cook for 2 minutes. Stir in the chopped tomatoes and the liquid from the pepper jar, followed by the sliced peppers and lentils. Season with salt and pepper and give everything a good stir, then cook for 12 minutes, stirring occasionally.

4. Make 4 indentations in the sauce with the back of a large spoon and crack an egg into each. As you add them to the hot sauce, the eggs should hold their shape but don't worry if one breaks or sinks as it will still all taste delicious! Cover the pan with a lid if you have one and cook for about 10 minutes or until the egg whites are just set.

5. Serve topped with the yoghurt or labneh, the crumbled feta and chopped parsley. Accompany with toasted sourdough bread.

SMOKED HADDOCK & GLORIOUS GRAIN KEDGEREE

A mildly spiced Anglo-Indian dish that was a staple part of every hearty Victorian breakfast both in India and back home in Britain. Traditionally made with rice, this recipe uses grains instead and, combined with the poached smoked haddock and boiled eggs, it is comfort food at its very best. As well as serving for breakfast or brunch, the kedgeree also works well as a light supper dish.

  SERVES 2   25 MINS

INGREDIENTS
- 2 free-range eggs
- 150g or 1 small fillet of smoked haddock
- 1 onion
- 3 cloves of garlic
- 2 tbsp olive oil
- 1 tbsp fresh or dried curry leaves
- 1 tsp ground cumin
- 1 tsp ground coriander
- 1 tsp ground turmeric
- ½ tsp black mustard seeds
- 1 x 250g pouch of ready cooked Glorious Grains with Red Rice & Quinoa
- 50g cooked fresh or frozen peas
- chilli sauce, to serve (optional)

METHOD
1. Bring a saucepan of water to the boil, carefully lower in the eggs and boil for 7 minutes. Immediately scoop them out of the water and run under cold water for a couple of minutes.

2. While the eggs are cooking, put the haddock in another pan, cover it with cold water, put a lid on the pan and poach for about 4 minutes. Drain the fish and gently break the flesh into large flakes, discarding the skin. When the eggs are ready, peel and cut them in half. Set aside.

3. Peel and finely chop the onion and garlic. Heat the oil in a large frying pan over a medium heat, add the onion and garlic and fry for 2 minutes or until translucent.

4. Add the curry leaves, cumin, coriander, turmeric and mustard seeds and fry for a few minutes to release their fragrant aroma. Stir in the grains and cook for 5 minutes. Add a splash of water and then stir in the peas, fish and eggs. Cook gently for about 5 minutes to heat everything through.

5. Divide the kedgeree between serving plates and serve immediately, with chilli sauce if you like.

CHESTNUT WAFFLES

These beautifully light waffles are crisp on the outside, soft and fluffy on the inside and contain chunks of chopped chestnut that add a crumbly texture and a sweet flavour. The waffles can be served with savoury or sweet toppings.

 SERVES 6   30 MINS   VEGETARIAN

INGREDIENTS

For the waffle batter
- 250g plain flour
- 1 tsp baking powder
- ½ tsp salt
- 1 tsp caster sugar
- 400ml milk
- 3 free-range eggs, separated
- 1 x 180g pouch of ready roasted Whole Chestnuts

METHOD

1. To make the waffle batter, sift the flour and baking powder into a mixing bowl and stir in the salt and sugar.

2. Whisk together the milk and egg yolks.

3. Gradually whisk the milk and yolks into the dry ingredients until you have a smooth batter. If making savoury waffles, add the chives and paprika.

4. Roughly chop the chestnuts and fold them through the batter.

5. In another bowl, whisk the egg whites until standing in firm peaks. Gently fold them into the batter until evenly mixed in.

For savoury waffles
- 2 tbsp chopped fresh chives, plus extra for sprinkling
- 1 tsp paprika
- 6 poached eggs

For sweet waffles
- 3 bananas, sliced
- 6 tbsp chocolate and hazelnut spread
- 3 tbsp maple syrup

6. Heat a waffle maker and pour in some of the batter. Close the lid and cook for about 4 minutes or until you have a crisp, golden waffle. Use the rest of the batter to cook 5 more waffles.

7. To serve, top the savoury waffles with poached eggs and a sprinkling of chopped chives. Top the sweet waffles with banana slices, generous spoonfuls of chocolate and hazelnut spread and a drizzle of maple syrup.

Snacks

SMOKY SPANISH-STYLE GRAIN EMPANADAS WITH ROASTED PEPPERS & CHEESE

These two-bite empanadas made with crisp, melt-in-the-mouth pastry have a delicious filling of roasted peppers, smoky Spanish-style grains & rice, and melted cheese. If you're pushed for time or don't fancy yourself as a pastry chef, you can buy ready-made shortcrust or puff pastry.

 MAKES 16 SMALL OR 8 LARGE   1 HR   Ⓥ VEGETARIAN

INGREDIENTS

For the pastry
- 360g plain flour, plus extra for kneading and rolling out
- 1 tsp salt
- 60g frozen butter, grated
- 1 free-range egg, beaten

For the filling
- 1 tbsp olive oil
- 1 onion, chopped
- 2 cloves of garlic
- 1 tsp smoked paprika
- ½ red chilli, deseeded and finely chopped
- a handful of young spinach leaves, chopped
- 2 flame-roasted red peppers, deseeded and chopped
- 1 x 250g pouch of ready cooked Smoky Spanish-style Grains & Rice
- 200g cheese of your choice (e.g. feta, mozzarella, Cheddar), diced
- 1 free-range egg yolk
- 1 tbsp milk
- salt

METHOD

1. To make the pastry, sift the flour and salt into a mixing bowl and rub in the butter until the mixture is like fine breadcrumbs. Stir in the beaten egg and gradually add 300ml cold water until the mixture comes together into a soft dough. Knead lightly for 2–3 minutes on a floured surface until the dough is smooth.

2. Roll out the pastry to 4mm thick and stamp out 16 rounds using a 15cm round cutter or plate. Lift the rounds onto 2 baking trays lined with baking parchment and chill in the fridge for 30 minutes to give the pastry time to relax and firm up.

3. To make the filling, heat the oil in a frying pan and fry the onion and garlic for 2 minutes until softened. Add the paprika and chilli, followed by the spinach and chopped red peppers. When the spinach has wilted, remove the pan from the heat, stir in the grains and rice and cheese and set aside to cool.

4. Preheat the oven to 220°C (200°C fan)/Gas mark 7. Remove the pastry rounds from the fridge and divide the filling between them, spooning the filling onto one half of each round.

5. Brush the pastry edges lightly with water and fold the pastry over the filling to enclose it. Crimp the pastry edges with your fingers or by pressing them together with a fork so the empanadas are tightly sealed. Beat together the egg yolk and milk and brush over the pastry. Sprinkle with salt.

6. Bake in the oven for 20–25 minutes until the pastry is golden brown and crisp. Serve the empanadas hot or warm.

BEETROOT, CUMIN & LENTIL HUMMUS WITH CRISP TORTILLA WEDGES & CRUNCHY VEGETABLES

This colourful dip makes a satisfying snack when you want something quick. You could also serve it as part of a buffet spread. If serving for a party, spoon it into a serving bowl and arrange wedges of tortilla and raw vegetables around it as dippers.

 SERVES 2-4   15 MINS   (VE) VEGAN

INGREDIENTS

For the beetroot & cumin hummus
- 2 tsp cumin seeds
- 300g cooked beetroot, peeled and roughly chopped
- ½ x 250g pouch of ready cooked Champagne Lentils
- 2 tbsp tahini
- 1 clove of garlic
- 1 tbsp olive oil
- 1 tbsp chopped fresh dill, plus extra for sprinkling
- juice of 1 lemon
- salt and black pepper

To serve
- 2 tortilla flatbreads
- 1 tbsp olive oil
- raw mixed vegetables

METHOD

1. To make the beetroot & cumin hummus, toast the cumin seeds in a dry frying pan to release their aroma. Set 1 teaspoon of the seeds aside.

2. Blend the remaining cumin seeds with the beetroot, lentils, tahini, garlic, olive oil and dill until you have a smooth purée. Add the lemon juice, season with salt and pepper and blend again. If the mixture is a little too thick, add a splash of water and blend until it is the right consistency.

3. When ready to serve, preheat the oven to 190°C (170°C fan)/Gas mark 5. Cut each tortilla into 8 wedges, place on a baking sheet and drizzle with the olive oil. Season with salt and bake in the oven for 10 minutes until crisp.

4. Swirl the hummus attractively on a large plate and sprinkle with extra dill and the reserved cumin seeds. Accompany with the tortilla wedges and raw vegetables.

CHARRED AUBERGINE & TAHINI DIP WITH CRISPY SPICED LENTILS

Scorching the aubergines over a gas flame or roasting them on a barbecue gives them a distinctive smoky flavour. You could get a similar effect by grilling but, while the smokiness would be less pronounced, the dip would taste equally good. The jerk chickpea recipe (see page 44) would also work well as a topping for the aubergine dip.

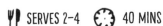 SERVES 2–4   40 MINS   (V) VEGETARIAN

INGREDIENTS

For the crispy lentils
- ½ x 250g pouch of ready cooked Champagne Lentils
- finely grated zest of ½ lemon
- 2 cloves of garlic, grated
- 1 tbsp olive oil
- 1 tbsp roughly chopped fresh flat-leaf parsley
- salt and black pepper

For the aubergine dip
- 2 aubergines
- 1 clove of garlic, peeled
- juice of 1 lemon
- 2 tbsp tahini
- 1 tbsp natural yoghurt

METHOD

1. To make the crispy lentils, preheat the oven to 220°C (200°C fan)/Gas mark 7.

2. Line a roasting tin with baking parchment, empty the lentils into it and sprinkle with the lemon zest and garlic. Drizzle with olive oil, season with salt and pepper and mix well. Cook in the oven for 20 minutes and then set aside to cool. When the lentils are cold, stir in the chopped parsley.

3. Prepare the aubergine dip. If you have a gas hob, grip the aubergines, one at a time, with tongs and hold them over the flame until the skin is charred, turning them regularly so they are blackened all over and are completely collapsed and soft. This should take about 8 minutes for each aubergine. Alternatively, barbecue the aubergines or grill them in a roasting tin under a high heat for 20 minutes, turning them over occasionally.

4. Set the aubergines aside until cool enough to handle, then cut them in half lengthways. Using a spoon, scrape out the soft flesh inside into a blender and add the garlic, lemon juice, tahini and yoghurt. Blend until smooth.

5. Spread the aubergine mixture into a shallow dish and spoon over the lentils.

To make this vegan: use dairy-free yoghurt.

ROASTED 'JERK' CHICKPEAS & LENTILS

This spicy blend of lentils and chickpeas is ideal for snacking when you're on the move. It also makes a great topping for salads, dips, rice pilafs or even stews. If you haven't got all the spices, you can substitute bought jerk seasoning.

 SERVES 2   40 MINS   (VE) VEGAN

INGREDIENTS

- 1 x 250g pouch of ready cooked Puy Lentils
- 1 x 400g can of chickpeas, drained and rinsed
- 1 tbsp demerara sugar
- 1 tsp salt
- 1 tsp ground allspice
- ½ tsp chilli powder
- 1 tsp ground cumin
- 1 tsp garlic granules
- 1 tsp paprika
- ½ tsp ground turmeric
- 2 tbsp olive oil

METHOD

1. Preheat the oven to 200°C (180°C fan)/Gas mark 6. Line a baking tray with baking parchment.

2. Mix all the ingredients together in a large bowl, making sure the lentils and chickpeas are well coated in the sugar, spices and oil. Tip the mixture into the baking tray, spreading it out in a thin layer so it dries out quickly and evenly and doesn't clump together.

3. Roast in the oven for 30–35 minutes or until almost dry. Remove and set aside to cool on the tray — the lentils and chickpeas will crisp up when cold. Store in an airtight container and eat within 3 days.

ROSEMARY, FENNEL & LENTIL CRACKERS

Store these crackers in an airtight container to keep them fresh, as they will be a great standby when you come home craving something to keep the hunger pangs at bay. Serve with a vegan dip, or some cheese if you are vegetarian.

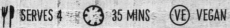 **SERVES 4** · **35 MINS** · **VE VEGAN**

INGREDIENTS
- 150g dried Puy Lentils
- ½ tsp salt
- 2 tbsp fresh rosemary leaves
- 2 tbsp flaxseeds
- ½ tsp fennel seeds
- 100g plain flour, plus extra for dusting
- 2 tbsp olive oil
- Maldon sea salt, for sprinkling
- shaved fennel and vegan dips, to serve

METHOD
1. Preheat the oven to 190°C (170°C fan)/Gas mark 5.

2. Grind the dried lentils, salt, 1 tablespoon of the rosemary, 1 tablespoon of the flaxseeds and the fennel seeds to a fine flour. Sift the flour into a bowl and stir in the lentil mixture.

3. Add the remaining flaxseeds, finely chop the remaining rosemary and stir in with the olive oil. Add 100ml cold water, stir and then knead everything together for about 2 minutes to make a soft dough.

4. Line a baking tray with baking parchment. Roll out the dough as thinly as possible on the baking parchment. The thinner you can roll it, the more like a cracker than a biscuit it will be when baked. Sprinkle with Maldon sea salt.

5. Bake for about 20–25 minutes until golden. Transfer to a wire rack and leave to cool. The baked dough will become crisper once it is cold. Break into pieces and serve with some shaved fennel and vegan dips.

SMOKY TOMATOEY LENTIL PÂTÉ WITH HERITAGE TOMATOES & BASIL

Serve this spicy, smoky spread on sourdough toast with tomatoes and fresh basil. Heritage – also called 'heirloom' – tomatoes are traditional varieties of tomato that were widely grown in the past, and then fell out of favour for a while, but fortunately are now being cultivated again by many growers. They come in a rainbow of colours, so not only are they big on flavour, they add a wonderful vibrancy to a salad.

 SERVES 2   25 MINS   VEGETARIAN

INGREDIENTS

For the smoky tomatoey lentil pâté
- 1 x 250g pouch of ready cooked Tomatoey French Puy & Green Lentils
- 100g full-fat cream cheese
- 1 tbsp sun-dried tomato purée
- 1 tsp chipotle chilli paste
- salt and black pepper

To serve
- 2 tbsp olive oil
- 4 slices of sourdough bread
- 2 cloves of garlic
- 100g heritage tomatoes
- a handful of fresh basil leaves

METHOD

1. To make the smoky tomatoey lentil pâté, blend the lentils, cream cheese, sun-dried tomato purée, chilli paste and 4 teaspoons water together to make a thick paste. Season with salt and pepper.

2. To serve, heat the oil in a frying pan and fry the slices of bread in the pan until they are golden and lightly scorched on both sides.

3. Peel the garlic cloves and rub 1 clove over the bread slices. Crush the other clove with a little salt and put it in a bowl. Slice the tomatoes and add to the bowl with half the torn basil leaves.

4. Spread the bread with the pâté and serve with the garlicky tomatoes and the remaining basil scattered on top.

FRUIT, NUT & SUPER SEEDS GRANOLA BARS

A powerhouse of nutrition packed into a small bar! Make a batch of these granola bars to pop into the family's weekday lunch boxes as they head off to work or school.

 MAKES 14   40 MINS   (V) VEGETARIAN

INGREDIENTS

For the granola bars
- 1 x 250g pouch of ready cooked Super Seeds with Quinoa & Chia
- 50g buckwheat
- 120g mixed seeds (e.g. sesame, pumpkin, flaxseeds, sunflower)
- 1 tbsp chia seeds
- 30g spelt flakes
- 50g puffed buckwheat
- 130g pitted dates
- 3 tbsp runny honey or maple syrup
- 3 tbsp peanut butter

For the topping (optional)
- 50g dark chocolate, chopped and melted

METHOD

1. To make the granola bars, preheat the oven to 200°C (180°C fan)/Gas mark 6 and line a 30- x 20-cm baking tin with parchment paper.

2. Mix the super seeds, buckwheat, mixed seeds, chia seeds, spelt flakes and puffed buckwheat together in a mixing bowl.

3. Roughly chop the dates. Put them in a saucepan, add the honey or maple syrup and peanut butter and place over a medium heat until the honey or maple syrup and peanut butter have melted. The mixture will start to come together like a thick caramel, but stir it constantly for about 5 minutes so it doesn't burn.

4. Leave to cool slightly, then pour onto the seed mixture in the bowl. Stir until the seeds are thoroughly coated with the caramel.

5. Spoon the seed mixture into the prepared baking tin, pressing it out in an even layer with the back of the spoon.

6. Bake in the oven for 25 minutes. Leave to cool in the tin before cutting in half lengthways and then across into 7 to make 14 bars.

7. For a final flourish, you can drizzle melted chocolate over the bars, leaving them until the chocolate has almost set before removing from the baking tin.

To make this vegan: *Use maple syrup instead of honey, and omit the chocolate or use a vegan one.*

CHESTNUT, CHOCOLATE & OAT ENERGY BITES

These chewy bites will keep your energy reserves topped up when you're having a tough day. Containing no added sugar but full of good things like oats and seeds, they include a little dark chocolate for an extra pick-me-up.

MAKES 16 · **10 MINS** · **(V) VEGETARIAN**

INGREDIENTS
- 100g dark chocolate
- 1 x 180g pouch of ready roasted Whole Chestnuts
- 200g pitted dates
- 60g jumbo rolled oats
- 2 tbsp flaxseeds

METHOD
1. Chop the chocolate and melt it in a heatproof bowl over a pan of simmering water, making sure the bottom of the bowl doesn't touch the water, or on the 'defrost' setting in the microwave. Stir until the chocolate is smooth and glossy.

2. Put the chestnuts, dates, oats and flaxseeds in a food processor and pulse to reduce them to chunky crumbs.

3. Transfer the crumbs to a bowl and stir in the melted chocolate. Shape the mixture into 16 discs with your hands.

4. Store in the fridge for up to 1 week – if they last that long!

To make this vegan: use vegan dark chocolate.

TROPICAL TRAIL MIX

A totally moreish snack that you won't be able to stop nibbling! The recipe features chestnuts dipped in dark chocolate to give a lovely texture that is perfect with chewy dried fruit.

SERVES 4–6 · **40 MINS** · **(V) VEGETARIAN**

INGREDIENTS
- 100g dark chocolate
- 1 x 180g pouch of ready roasted Whole Chestnuts, roughly chopped
- 100g dried banana chips
- 100g dried mango pieces
- 40g goji berries
- 60g pecans
- 25g coconut flakes

1. Line a baking tray with baking parchment.

2. Chop the chocolate and melt it as described in the recipe above.

3. Stir the chopped chestnuts into the melted chocolate until well coated. Set the chestnuts on the baking tray and, when cool, put in the fridge to set.

4. Mix the remaining ingredients together. When the chocolate has set, add the chestnuts to the mix.

5. Store in sealed bags or jars for up to 1 week.

To make this vegan: use vegan dark chocolate.

WHOLEMEAL RYE & GRAIN SODA BREAD

This wholemeal soda bread is packed with all kinds of good things. As the dough doesn't require proving, the bread is quick and easy to make, and you can ring the changes by adding different grains and other flavourings. Toast the bread and spread it with butter and jam, or eat as an accompaniment to a ploughman's lunch with cheese and salad.

 MAKES 1 LOAF 45 MINS Ⓥ VEGETARIAN

INGREDIENTS
- 300g wholemeal self-raising flour, plus 75g extra for dusting
- 50g rye flour
- 1 tsp bicarbonate of soda
- 1 tsp salt
- 1 x 250g pouch of ready cooked Glorious Grains with Red Rice & Quinoa
- 50g sun-dried tomatoes, chopped
- 2 tbsp pumpkin seeds
- 1 free-range egg
- 300g natural yoghurt
- 1 tbsp poppy seeds

METHOD
1. Preheat the oven to 240°C (220°C fan)/Gas mark 8. Line a baking tray with baking parchment.

2. In a large mixing bowl, mix together the 300g wholemeal flour, the rye flour, bicarbonate of soda and salt.

3. Stir in the grains, chopped sun-dried tomatoes and pumpkin seeds.

4. Beat together the egg and yoghurt and mix into the flour mixture, along with 1 tablespoon of the pumpkin seeds.

5. Stir with a wooden spoon until everything is combined, then tip the dough onto a work surface dusted with a little flour – the dough will be very wet at this point.

6. Sprinkle over the remaining 75g wholemeal flour and slowly knead this in. Shape the dough into a ball and place it on the baking tray.

7. Press the poppy seeds and the remaining pumpkin seeds over the dough and, using a sharp knife, score a criss-cross pattern in the top. Bake in the oven for 35 minutes, or until the loaf is golden brown and it sounds hollow when the base is lightly tapped. Leave to cool on a wire rack.

HERBY LENTIL & MUSTARD SCOTCH EGGS WITH A GARLIC MAYONNAISE DIP

These herby vegetarian alternatives to classic Scotch eggs are made with peppery Beluga® lentils and potato, and have a warm mustard kick. Eat them warm with a salad or leave them to cool and pack them into a picnic basket.

 **MAKES 3**   **1 HR**   Ⓥ **VEGETARIAN**

INGREDIENTS

For the Scotch eggs
- 1 large potato, peeled and diced
- 4 free-range eggs
- 1 x 250g pouch of ready cooked Beluga® Lentils
- 1 clove of garlic
- 2 tbsp coarsely chopped fresh flat-leaf parsley
- 2 tbsp coarsely chopped fresh chives
- 2 tsp Dijon mustard
- 2–3 tbsp plain flour
- 150g panko (dry breadcrumbs)
- vegetable oil for deep-frying
- salt and black pepper

For the garlic mayonnaise dip
- 2 cloves of garlic
- 4 tbsp mayonnaise

METHOD

1. To make the Scotch eggs, put the diced potato in a pan and cover with cold water. Add a pinch of salt, bring the water to the boil and cook until the chunks of potato are tender when pierced with the point of a knife. Drain and set aside.

2. Cook 3 of the eggs in a pan of simmering water for 6 minutes, drain and run under cold water for a couple of minutes. Peel and set aside.

3. Put half the lentils, the garlic, parsley, chives, mustard and potatoes in a food processor and season with salt and pepper. Blitz until you get a paste (or finely chop everything by hand). Empty it into a bowl and stir in the rest of the lentils.

4. Flatten one-third of the lentil mixture into a disc in your hand, put a peeled egg in the centre and wrap it around the egg to enclose. Repeat with the remaining mixture and eggs.

5. Spread the flour on a plate, beat the remaining egg in a shallow bowl and spread the panko breadcrumbs on another plate. Roll the wrapped eggs in the flour, brush with beaten egg and roll in the breadcrumbs until coated. Give the eggs a second coating of beaten egg and breadcrumbs, rolling them gently between your palms to stick any loose crumbs in place. Refrigerate for at least 30 minutes for the coating to firm up.

6. Meanwhile, make the garlic mayonnaise dip by peeling and crushing the garlic and stirring it into the mayonnaise.

7. Heat the oil for deep-frying to 170°C and deep-fry the eggs for about 5 minutes, or until golden brown and crisp. Drain on a plate lined with kitchen paper, then serve with the dip.

Lunch on the Go

SMOKY SPANISH FRITTATA WITH SPINACH, PEPPER & FETA

This Spanish-style omelette is a versatile dish as it can be served hot straight from the pan with a salad if you're eating at home, or left to cool and then packed into lunch boxes or a picnic hamper.

 SERVES 6-8 15 MINS

INGREDIENTS

- 6 free-range eggs
- 1 x 250g pouch of ready cooked Smoky Spanish-style Grains & Rice
- 100g baby spinach leaves, chopped
- a pinch of dried chilli flakes
- 2 tbsp olive oil
- 100g chorizo, sliced
- 1 red pepper, deseeded and sliced
- 70g feta
- salt and black pepper

METHOD

1. Preheat the oven to 190°C (170°C fan)/Gas mark 5.

2. Beat the eggs in a large bowl, then whisk in the grains and rice, spinach and chilli flakes. Season with salt and pepper.

3. Heat the oil in a large ovenproof frying pan, add the sliced chorizo and red pepper and fry for 2 minutes. Pour the egg mixture evenly into the pan and crumble over the feta.

4. Cook on the hob for 3–4 minutes, then transfer to the oven and bake for about 6 minutes until the eggs are just set.

5. Slide the frittata out of the pan onto a board and serve hot, cut into wedges, or transfer to a wire rack and leave to cool.

ROASTED CARROT, ROCKET & LENTIL SALAD

Roasting carrots brings out their sweet flavour, so this hearty salad will be equally popular with children and adults. Za'atar is a Middle Eastern blend that usually contains thyme, oregano, marjoram, sumac and sesame seeds.

SERVES 2   **25 MINS**   **(VE) VEGAN**

INGREDIENTS

- 300g carrots (if possible, use a mix of different coloured ones), washed
- 100ml olive oil
- 1 tbsp cumin seeds
- 1 tsp dried chilli flakes
- 1 tsp za'atar
- 2 tbsp pumpkin seeds
- 1 tbsp wholegrain mustard
- finely grated zest and juice of 1 lemon
- 1 x 250g pouch of ready cooked Beluga® Lentils
- 50g rocket
- 2 tbsp roughly chopped fresh dill
- salt and black pepper

METHOD

1. Preheat the oven to 200°C (180°C fan)/Gas mark 6.

2. Cut the carrots in half lengthways and spread them out in a roasting tin. Spoon half the olive oil over the carrots and turn them over so that they are well coated in oil.

3. Sprinkle the cumin seeds, chilli flakes and za'atar over the carrots and season with salt and pepper. Roast in the oven for 15–20 minutes until the carrots are tender and they are starting to turn golden at the edges. Add the pumpkin seeds for the last 3 minutes, so the seeds are lightly toasted.

4. Whisk the remaining olive oil, mustard, lemon zest and juice, and Beluga® lentils in a large bowl and season with salt and pepper. Add half the rocket and the dill and stir well to mix everything together.

5. Pile the remaining rocket on a large platter and top with the roasted carrots and dressed lentils.

RAINBOW JAR SALAD LAYERED WITH GRAINS, & GINGER & SESAME DRESSING

Salads needn't be boring, as this brightly layered mix of vegetables, grains and rice noodles proves. You'll need 2 glass preserving jars with wide mouths and screw or clip on lids, each large enough to take half the ingredients. Once you've layered the salads, pour over the punchy sesame dressing, screw or clip the lids firmly on the jars and your 'take-away' lunches (one for you and one for a friend!) will be the envy of everyone.

 SERVES 2   15 MINS   VEGETARIAN

INGREDIENTS

For the ginger & sesame dressing
- 4 tbsp sesame oil
- 2 tbsp soy sauce
- 2 tbsp honey
- 1 red chilli, deseeded
- 1 clove of garlic, peeled
- 1cm piece of root ginger, peeled

For the salad
- 1 carrot
- 6 cherry tomatoes
- 2 radishes
- 1 x 250g pouch of ready cooked Glorious Grains with Red Rice & Quinoa
- 100g edamame beans
- 100g cooked rice noodles
- 100g baby spinach leaves
- 2 tbsp chopped fresh coriander
- 20g mange tout
- sesame seeds, for sprinkling
- 1 lime

METHOD

1. To make the ginger & sesame dressing, whisk together the sesame oil, soy sauce and honey. Very finely chop the chilli and finely grate the garlic and ginger. Add to the soy sauce mixture and set aside.

2. To make the salad, peel the carrot and shave into ribbons with a vegetable peeler, or cut into thin strips or batons. Halve the cherry tomatoes and slice the radishes.

3. Now the layering begins! Start with the glorious grains, spooning those first into the jars so they will be at the bottom and can soak up the dressing. Layer the edamame beans, carrot, noodles, cherry tomatoes, radishes, spinach, coriander and mange tout on top.

4. Pour half the dressing into each jar and finish with a sprinkling of sesame seeds.

5. Cut the lime in half and place half on top of each salad, ready to squeeze over just before eating.

6. Seal the jars by screwing or clipping on the lids. When ready to eat, first push your fork to the bottom of the jar so you can muddle everything together.

To make this vegan: replace the honey with agave syrup.

QUINOA-CRUSTED QUICHE WITH CHEESE, MUSHROOMS & TRUFFLED LENTILS

If you follow a gluten-free diet, quiches are usually off the menu as the pastry contains flour. However, this is one quiche you can enjoy as its crust is made with baked quinoa spiced with nigella seeds. The flavour-packed filling is a mix of wild mushrooms, truffled lentils, mature Cheddar cheese and chives.

 SERVES 6–8   50 MINS   VEGETARIAN

INGREDIENTS

For the crust
- 1 x 250g pouch of ready cooked Red & White Quinoa
- 2 tsp nigella seeds
- 2 free-range egg whites

For the filling
- 1 clove of garlic
- 250g mixed wild mushrooms
- 1 tbsp olive oil
- 4 free-range eggs
- 200ml double cream
- 200g Cheddar cheese, grated
- 15g fresh chives, finely chopped, plus extra to serve
- 15g fresh dill, finely chopped, plus extra to serve
- 1 x 250g pouch of ready cooked Puglian Lentils with Truffle Infused Oil

METHOD

1. To make the crust, preheat the oven to 200°C (180°C fan)/ Gas mark 6. Grease a 23-cm loose-bottomed flan tin and place on a baking tray.

2. For the crust, mix the quinoa and nigella seeds together in a large bowl.

3. Whisk the egg whites into the quinoa and seeds.

4. Press the quinoa mixture into the flan tin over the base and up the sides in an even layer. Bake for 15 minutes or until the crust is set and crunchy.

5. To make the filling, chop the garlic finely and slice or chop the mushrooms, depending on their size. Heat the oil in a frying pan and quickly fry the garlic and mushrooms until golden and just cooked.

6. Whisk together the eggs, cream, cheese, chives, dill and lentils. Spoon the mushrooms into the quinoa case and carefully pour over the egg mixture.

7. Return the quiche to the oven and bake for 20 minutes, or until the filling is just set but still has a slight wobble.

8. Serve warm or cold, with extra herbs on top.

A WARMING BOWL OF SWEET POTATO, LENTIL, COCONUT & GINGER SOUP

On a cold day, this hearty soup made with a mix of vegetables, lentils, spices and coconut can be relied on to warm you up. The oven-roasted vegetables and lentils are blended with the spices and coconut milk to produce a nourishing and fragrantly-scented, thick broth.

 SERVES 2-4 30 MINS VEGAN

INGREDIENTS
- 500g sweet potatoes
- 2 carrots
- 1 red onion
- 2 cloves of garlic
- 1 red chilli
- 1 tbsp melted coconut oil
- 1 x 400g can of coconut milk
- 2.5cm piece of root ginger, peeled
- 1 lemon grass stalk
- 1 x 250g pouch of ready cooked Puy Lentils
- salt and black pepper
- fresh coriander leaves, to serve
- olive oil, for drizzling

METHOD
1. Preheat the oven to 200°C (180°C fan)/Gas mark 6.

2. Peel the sweet potatoes and carrots and cut into roughly 2.5cm cubes. Peel and chop the onion and garlic and slice the chilli, removing the seeds if preferred. Toss the vegetables with the coconut oil, season and spread out in a roasting tin. Cook in the oven for 20 minutes, or until the vegetables are tender.

3. Pour the coconut milk and 400ml water into a large saucepan. Chop the ginger, crush the lemon grass stalk and add both to the pan. Stir in the lentils and bring to a gentle simmer.

4. When the vegetables are ready, set aside one quarter of them for topping the finished soup. Remove and discard the lemon grass from the coconut milk mixture and blend with the remaining vegetables until smooth.

5. When ready to serve, reheat the soup and reserved vegetables. Ladle the hot soup into serving bowls and top with the vegetables, coriander and a drizzle of olive oil.

CHARGRILLED PEACH, FREEKEH & PROSCIUTTO SALAD WITH MINT & ALMOND

Sweet chargrilled peaches and salty prosciutto make a winning combination in this satisfying salad. Almonds and buckwheat contribute a nutty flavour, while the freekeh adds texture. Freekeh is a green durum wheat that has been roasted to give it a smoky flavour and it is rich in fibre and protein. If you've never tried adding it to a salad before, this recipe will convince you how well it works with other ingredients. To ring the changes, the salad can be topped with a mild, soft cheese, such as burrata or mozzarella.

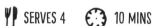 SERVES 4   10 MINS

INGREDIENTS

For the salad
- 4 fresh peaches
- 1 tbsp olive oil
- 1 x 250g pouch of ready cooked Freekeh
- 1 tbsp toasted buckwheat
- 30g whole blanched almonds
- 2 tbsp fresh mint leaves
- 8 slices of prosciutto

For the dressing
- 2 tsp pomegranate molasses
- 1 tbsp sherry vinegar
- 4 tsp olive oil
- salt and black pepper

METHOD

1. Preheat a ridged grill pan or cast iron frying pan over a high heat.

2. While the pan is heating, halve the peaches and remove the stones. Spoon the oil onto a large plate and dip the cut sides of the peaches in the oil. Lay them, cut side down, on the hot grill pan.

3. Put the freekeh, buckwheat, almonds and mint leaves on a serving platter, reserving the prosciutto for topping the salad.

4. To make the dressing, whisk all the ingredients together and spoon half over the freekeh mixture.

5. Check the peaches and if the cut sides are attractively marked with scorch lines, they are ready. Lift them out of the pan with a spatula and leave them on the oiled plate to cool. Pour a little of the remaining dressing over them to mix with the juices from the peaches.

6. Arrange the prosciutto slices and peach halves over the salad on the platter and drizzle any juices from the peaches and the remaining dressing over. Serve immediately.

MISO & HONEY ROASTED AUBERGINE WITH CORIANDER & SESAME QUINOA SALAD

Roasting an aubergine in miso – a fermented rice and soya bean paste that is widely used in Japanese cuisine – gives it a unique sweet-savoury flavour. Served with a coriander, sesame and quinoa salad, this makes an unusual lunch dish for anyone who enjoys Asian food.

 SERVES 2 30 MINS Ⓥ VEGETARIAN

INGREDIENTS

For the aubergine
- 1 aubergine
- 2 tbsp white miso paste
- 2 tbsp runny honey
- 1 tbsp mirin (Japanese rice wine)
- 1 tbsp soy sauce
- 4 tsp sesame oil

For the coriander & sesame quinoa salad
- 1 x 250g pouch of ready cooked Red & White Quinoa
- a handful of baby kale leaves
- 2 tbsp chopped fresh coriander
- 2 tbsp light olive oil
- 1 lime, cut in half
- salt and black pepper
- 1 tbsp sesame seeds, to serve

METHOD

1. To cook the aubergine, preheat the oven to 200°C (180°C fan)/Gas mark 6.

2. Cut the aubergine into quarters lengthways, score the flesh with a sharp knife and put the quarters in a roasting tin.

3. Mix together the miso paste, honey, mirin, soy sauce and sesame oil and rub or brush the mixture all over the aubergine quarters. (Reserve any leftover miso dressing for later.) Roast them in the oven for 25 minutes or until golden and crisp at the edges.

4. To prepare the coriander & sesame quinoa salad, empty the quinoa into a bowl and add the baby kale, coriander and olive oil. Season and squeeze over the juice from one half of the lime. Stir in any remaining miso dressing.

5. To serve, divide the salad between serving plates and arrange 2 quarters of aubergine on each. Cut the remaining lime half into 2 wedges to squeeze over and sprinkle with the sesame seeds.

To make this vegan: replace the honey with agave syrup.

PANZANELLA WITH PESTO-EY GRAINS

Panzanella is a classic salad from Tuscany that's made with the freshest, ripest tomatoes, aromatic basil leaves, lightly pickled onions and crunchy croutons. It's useful for finishing up that half-eaten loaf that's gone stale in the bread bin, turning it into croutons that will soak up all the delicious tomato and vinegar juices in the salad bowl. The flavours go brilliantly with our pesto-ey grains. Use a variety of colours and types of tomato so the salad looks its most striking.

 SERVES 4   10 MINS   VEGETARIAN

INGREDIENTS

- 400g tomatoes (use different colours and varieties, if possible)
- 5 tbsp extra virgin olive oil, plus extra to drizzle
- 1 red onion
- 4 tbsp red wine vinegar
- 1 tsp salt
- ½ tsp sugar
- 30g stale bread
- 1 x 250g pouch of ready cooked Pesto-ey Italian-infused Grains
- 15g fresh basil leaves

METHOD

1. Cut the tomatoes into chunks of different shapes and sizes and place in a large bowl. Spoon over 4 tablespoons of the olive oil so the tomatoes are well coated.

2. Peel and thinly slice the onion. Separate the layers and spread them out in a small dish. Spoon over the vinegar, ½ teaspoon of the salt and the sugar.

3. Cut the bread into roughly 2.5cm chunks.

4. Heat the remaining 1 tablespoon of olive oil in a large frying pan and fry the chunks of bread until they are golden and crisp. Sprinkle with the remaining salt.

5. Mix the onion and vinegar with the tomatoes and croutons. Mix the grains with the basil leaves, reserving a few leaves to garnish the salad.

6. Combine the tomato and grain mixtures and transfer to a serving dish. Add a good drizzle of olive oil and garnish with the reserved basil leaves.

SUPER SALAD BOWL WITH PESTO-EY GRAINS, & CASHEW & TAHINI DRESSING

One look at this vivid green vegetable salad with its rich, nutty, tahini dressing and you'll immediately want to eat it. Packed with nutrients and minerals, it's everything a salad should be – crunchy, fresh and utterly delicious.

 SERVES 2–3 10 MINS VEGETARIAN

INGREDIENTS

For the cashew & tahini dressing
- 20g cashews, roughly chopped
- 1 clove of garlic, peeled
- juice of ½ lemon
- 2 tbsp tahini
- 15g fresh mint leaves
- 4 tsp olive oil

For the salad
- 80g kale, chopped
- juice of ½ lemon
- 1 apple
- 1 courgette
- 4 tbsp beetroot hummus (see page 40 for homemade)
- 1 x 250g pouch of ready cooked Pesto-ey Italian-infused Grains
- 80g broccoli, blanched and divided into small florets
- 40g edamame beans
- handful of salad sprouts
- 60g cashews, toasted
- 1 tbsp black sesame seeds

METHOD

1. To make the cashew & tahini dressing, blend all the ingredients in a blender with 2 teaspoons water until smooth.

2. To make the salad, toss the kale in a large bowl with 1 tablespoon of the lemon juice. Core and cut the apple into matchsticks. Dress with the remaining lemon juice to prevent the apple turning brown.

3. Grate or spiralize the courgette.

4. To assemble the salad, divide the beetroot hummus between individual serving bowls and arrange the salad ingredients on top. Start with the grains and then add the other vegetables in any order you wish.

5. Scatter over the toasted cashews and sesame seeds and pour over the dressing just before serving.

MUJADARA WITH PISTACHIO, ROSE PETALS & BARBERRIES

Mujadara is a Middle Eastern dish made with lentils and usually rice. This recipe is made with Champagne lentils, garnished with plenty of fried onions, can be served hot or cold, and includes pistachios and rose petals to add fragrance and crunch. It can also be served as an elegant side dish to slow-roasted joints of meat. You can buy most of the more interesting ingredients from Lebanese or Turkish shops. The crispy onions may seem a bit of an effort but they are incredibly addictive and can be added to all sorts of salads

 SERVES 4   35 MINS   VEGAN

INGREDIENTS

For the mujadara
- 2 onions
- 750ml vegetable oil
- 50g basmati rice
- 15g fresh flat-leaf parsley
- 25g shelled pistachios
- 1 x 250g pouch of ready cooked Champagne Lentils
- 1 lemon
- 2 tbsp edible dried rose petals
- 25g sultanas
- 2 tbsp barberries
- 2 tbsp pomegranate seeds
- salt and black pepper

For the salad box, per serving
- 4 batons of cucumber
- ¼ red pepper, sliced
- 2 raw broccoli florets
- 2 tbsp hummus
- 3–4 falafel (make sure they are vegan)

METHOD

1. Peel and finely slice the onions. Heat the oil in a large pan over a low heat. After about 5 minutes, when the oil shimmers, add the onions and cook, stirring frequently, for about 10 minutes, or until they are golden brown. Make sure you keep stirring. Using a slotted spoon, remove them from the pan and drain them on a plate lined with kitchen paper. Season with salt and pepper. You can leave the oil to cool and use it again for deep frying another time.

2. Cook the rice according to the instructions on the packet and leave to cool.

3. Roughly chop the parsley and pistachios.

4. Mix the cooled rice with the lentils, season and squeeze over the juice of the lemon. Add the rose petals, sultanas, barberries and pomegranate seeds.

5. Serve the mujadara with the cucumber, pepper, broccoli, hummus and falafel in a salad box.

HOT-SMOKED SALMON WITH QUINOA, COURGETTE & SPINACH

Red and white quinoa served with flakes of hot-smoked salmon and courgette 'spaghetti' ensures this lunch dish is a feast for the eyes as well as the palate. Add crunchy seeds, baby spinach and a tangy roasted lemon dressing and, while you'll have a dish that might be quick and easy to prepare, it's also special enough to serve if you're entertaining friends. If you don't have a spiralizer, bags of long, thin ropes of spiralized courgette can be bought ready prepared from supermarkets.

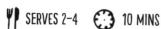 SERVES 2–4 10 MINS

INGREDIENTS
- 2 lemons
- 1 clove of garlic
- 2 tbsp olive oil
- 1 x 250g pouch of ready cooked Red & White Quinoa
- 225g hot-smoked salmon
- 25g baby spinach leaves
- 200g courgettes
- 20g mixed seeds (e.g. sunflower, pumpkin)

METHOD
1. Place a ridged grill pan over a high heat. Cut the lemons in half and put in the pan, cut side down. Leave until the flesh is charred, sticky and blackened.

2. Carefully lift the lemons out of the pan using tongs and, when cool enough to handle, squeeze out the juice through a sieve into a small bowl.

3. Grate or crush the garlic into the lemon juice and whisk in the olive oil.

4. Empty the quinoa onto plates and crumble it with your hands to break up any lumps.

5. Remove any skin from the salmon, flake the flesh into large chunks and add to a salad bowl along with the spinach leaves. Put the courgettes through a spiralizer and add them to the bowl as well. Pour over the dressing and mix well.

6. Spoon the salad over the quinoa and sprinkle over the mixed seeds before serving.

MIX-&-MATCH SALADS

If you think the best salads are time-consuming and complicated to make, the simple step-by-step guide overleaf, showing you how to select and assemble ingredients for a great salad, is just for you. Not only do the steps help you mix and match textures and flavours, they are also the perfect way to use up any leftovers that are lingering in the chiller drawer of the fridge.

To build your own salad, begin with a grain, add a vegetable, followed by a fresh herb, don't forget something crunchy and, finally, toss everything in a tangy dressing to bring all the different elements together.

First of all, you'll need a salad bowl large enough for all your chosen ingredients. Now, all you do is select one ingredient from each step to add to the bowl...

MIX-&-MATCH SALADS...

 SERVES 2   15–30 MINS   VEGETARIAN

STEP 1: CHOOSE YOUR GRAIN
- ready cooked Smoky Spanish-style Grains & Rice
- ready cooked Spicy Mexican-style Grains & Pulses
- ready cooked Pesto-ey Italian-infused Grains
- ready cooked Puy Lentils

STEP 2: CHOOSE YOUR VEGETABLE
- raw green, red or orange/yellow peppers, deseeded and sliced
- avocado, stoned, peeled and flesh sliced
- courgette, sliced and chargrilled
- butternut squash, peeled, deseeded, cut into chunks and roasted

STEP 3: CHOOSE YOUR HERB
(WHICH MUST BE FRESH NOT DRIED)
- flat-leaf parsley
- coriander
- basil
- thyme

STEP 4: CHOOSE YOUR CRUNCH
- seeds (pumpkin, sunflower, flax)
- toasted tortilla flatbreads, cut into cubes or torn into strips
- toasted or fried bread croutons
- nuts (hazelnuts, cashews, almonds)

STEP 5: CHOOSE YOUR DRESSING (FOR EACH DRESSING, WHISK ALL THE INGREDIENTS TOGETHER UNTIL THEY ARE EVENLY COMBINED)

- GARLIC – ½ clove of garlic, peeled and grated; 2 tbsp olive oil; juice of ½ lemon; salt and black pepper

- JALAPEÑO – ½ jalapeño chilli, deseeded and grated; 2 tbsp olive oil; juice of ½ lime; salt and black pepper

- BASIL – 15g fresh basil, leaves picked off their stalks and chopped; 2 tbsp olive oil; salt and black pepper

- BALSAMIC – 1 tbsp balsamic vinegar; ½ clove of garlic, peeled and grated; 2 tbsp olive oil; salt and black pepper

Weekday Dinners

ROASTED RED PEPPERS STUFFED WITH SPANISH-STYLE GRAINS & RICE

These long, pointed red romano peppers are stuffed with rice and grains that are spiced with fiery harissa chilli paste. The sweetness of the peppers, the heat of the harissa and the cooling cream cheese and avocado all complement each other perfectly.

 SERVES 2–3 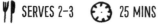 25 MINS VEGETARIAN

INGREDIENTS
- 3 long, red romano peppers
- 1 jalapeño chilli
- ½ red onion, peeled
- 1 x 250g pouch of ready cooked Smoky Spanish-style Grains & Rice
- 2 tbsp harissa
- 2 tbsp olive oil
- 2 tbsp cream cheese
- 1 avocado, peeled, stoned and roughly chopped
- finely grated zest and juice of 1 lime
- 25g fresh coriander leaves

METHOD
1. Preheat the oven to 200°C (180°C fan)/Gas mark 6.

2. Leave the stalks on the romano peppers, then cut a long slit through the peppers, lengthways, and remove the seeds. Lay them side by side in a roasting tin.

3. Finely chop the jalapeño chilli and red onion and stir into the Spanish-style grains & rice. Divide the rice mixture evenly between the peppers.

4. Mix the harissa and olive oil together and drizzle over the peppers, reserving a little for drizzling later. Roast in the oven for 15–20 minutes until the peppers are starting to char at the edges.

5. To serve, dot the cream cheese and avocado on top of the peppers. Sprinkle with the lime zest, squeeze over the juice, drizzle over the reserved harissa oil and finish with the coriander leaves.

LENTIL DHAL WITH PICKLED RED ONION, YOGHURT & CORIANDER

An Indian dhal is a slow-cooked lentil dish that would traditionally be gently simmered for at least 6 hours and even for as long as 24 hours. This is a cheat's version that only requires cooking for 30 minutes – a more practical option for today's busy lives – but made with Beluga® lentils and plenty of aromatic spices it's still an impressive dish.

 SERVES 2   35 MINS   VEGETARIAN

INGREDIENTS

For the lentil dhal
- 1 large onion
- 3 cloves of garlic
- 25g piece of root ginger
- 20g piece of turmeric root
- 2 tbsp butter or ghee
- 1 tsp garam masala
- 1 tsp ground turmeric
- 1 tsp ground coriander
- 1 tsp black mustard seeds
- 1 bay leaf
- 6 fresh or dried curry leaves (optional)
- 1 tbsp tomato purée
- 1 x 250g pouch of ready cooked Beluga® Lentils
- 500ml hot vegetable stock
- 2 tbsp double cream

For the pickled red onion
- 1 small red onion
- ½ salt
- 1 tsp sugar
- 2 tbsp white wine vinegar

To serve
- natural yoghurt
- chopped fresh coriander

METHOD

1. To make the lentil dhal, peel the onion, garlic, ginger and turmeric and chop them finely, or blend together in a small food processor with a little water to make a paste.

2. Melt the butter or ghee in a large saucepan and cook the onion mixture over a low heat for 3 minutes. Add the garam masala, ground turmeric, ground coriander, mustard seeds, bay leaf and curry leaves, if using. Fry for 2 minutes, then stir in the tomato purée and lentils.

3. Pour in the stock and simmer over a medium heat for 25 minutes, or until the stock has reduced and the lentil mixture is thick and creamy.

4. Meanwhile, to make the pickled red onion, peel and thinly slice the onion. Put it in a small bowl, add the salt, sugar and vinegar and stir well. Set aside to macerate and turn bright pink.

5. When the dhal is ready, stir in the cream.

6. Serve the dhal in bowls topped with natural yoghurt and plenty of chopped coriander, and the pickled red onion.

ROASTED CAULIFLOWER WITH LEMON COUSCOUS & TAHINI DRESSING

Roasting cauliflower as steaks makes it a much more interesting vegetable than simply boiling or steaming the florets; the cauliflower becomes lightly charred at the edges as it roasts, developing a warm, deeper flavour. Served with a Middle Eastern-style salad of wholewheat giant couscous and a tahini dressing, the dish can be eaten hot or cold.

 SERVES 2–4   30 MINS   VE VEGAN

INGREDIENTS

For the roasted cauliflower
- 1 cauliflower
- 2 tbsp olive oil
- 1 tsp sumac
- 1 tsp ground cumin
- 1 tsp garlic powder
- ½ tsp salt
- ½ tsp black pepper

For the lemon couscous
- 2 tbsp olive oil
- 300g dried Wholewheat Giant Couscous
- finely grated zest and juice of 1 lemon
- 1 tsp sumac
- seeds of 1 pomegranate
- 50g fresh mint leaves, picked from their stalks
- salt and black pepper

For the tahini dressing
- 2 tbsp tahini
- 2 cloves of garlic, peeled and crushed
- juice of ½ lemon

METHOD

1. To make the roasted cauliflower, preheat the oven to 190°C (170°C fan)/Gas mark 5. Line a baking tray with baking parchment.

2. Slice the cauliflower into 4 large steaks, brush them all over with the olive oil and sprinkle with the sumac, cumin and garlic powder. Season with the salt and pepper.

3. Lay the cauliflower steaks on the baking tray and roast for 15–20 minutes or until just tender and starting to char around the edges.

4. Meanwhile, prepare the lemon couscous. Heat the olive oil in a large frying pan, add the couscous and fry it for 2 minutes. Add 400ml water and simmer for 15 minutes until the couscous has absorbed the water and the grains are tender. Rinse under cold water and drain well.

5. Stir the lemon zest and juice and sumac into the couscous, followed by the pomegranate seeds and mint leaves, reserving a few of the seeds and leaves for garnish. Season.

6. To make the tahini dressing, in a small bowl, mix together the tahini and crushed garlic. Gradually whisk in 2 tablespoons water until the mixture has a creamy consistency. Add the lemon juice and season to taste.

7. Serve the lemon couscous with the cauliflower steaks on top. Drizzle over the tahini dressing and scatter over the reserved pomegranate seeds and mint leaves.

COD, BASIL & TOMATO BAKE WITH PESTO-EY GRAINS

We've used cod in this recipe but other fish fillets such as hake or salmon would work equally well. Roasted vine tomatoes and a quick, easy-to-make pesto are all that's needed to turn a simple fish dish into a sophisticated feast.

 SERVES 2   25 MINS

INGREDIENTS
- 1 x 250g pouch of ready cooked Pesto-ey Italian-infused Grains
- 25g fresh basil, leaves and stalks separated
- 2 tbsp olive oil
- 280g cod loin steak, cut into 2 fillets
- 300g mixed vine tomatoes
- leaves from 1 sprig of fresh thyme
- salt and black pepper

METHOD
1. Preheat the oven to 190°C (170°C fan)/Gas mark 5.

2. Spread out the pesto grains in an even layer in an ovenproof dish so that they cover the bottom of the dish, reserving 2 tablespoons.

3. Put the reserved grains into a small blender, add half the basil leaves and all the stalks. Add 4 teaspoons of the olive oil and blend to make a chunky pesto.

4. Lift the cod steaks into the ovenproof dish, on top of the grains. Arrange the tomatoes around the fish, leaving them on their vines, as these will add flavour, but cutting any really large tomatoes in half.

5. Drizzle the remaining olive oil over the fish, sprinkle with the thyme leaves and season with salt and pepper.

6. Bake in the oven for 20 minutes until the flesh of the cod is just flaking apart. Drizzle the pesto over, garnish with the remaining basil leaves and serve at once.

SPAGHETTI WITH TOMATOEY LENTIL BOLOGNESE

Here is a rich tomato Bolognese sauce that's hearty and filling and one that will be enjoyed by vegans and meat eaters alike. The sauce can be used as the base for many other dishes.

 SERVES 2   30 MINS   VEGAN

INGREDIENTS
- 1 onion
- 1 small carrot
- 3 cloves of garlic
- 1 celery stick
- 2 tbsp olive oil
- sprig of fresh rosemary
- 1 bay leaf
- 1 x 400g can of chopped tomatoes
- 1 tbsp tomato purée
- 1 x 250g pouch of ready cooked Tomatoey French Puy & Green Lentils
- salt and black pepper

To serve
- 70–100g dried spaghetti per person
- bread
- grated Parmesan cheese (optional)

METHOD

1. Peel and finely dice the onion and carrot and peel and finely chop the garlic. Trim and finely dice the celery. Heat the olive oil in a large saucepan over a medium heat and fry the diced vegetables and the garlic for 3 minutes until softened.

2. Add the rosemary and bay leaf and season with salt and pepper.

3. Tip in the tomatoes, fill the can with water and pour this in as well.

4. Stir in the tomato purée and lentils and cook for 15–20 minutes, or until the sauce has thickened and it is a rich dark red colour.

5. To serve, cook the pasta in boiling water according to the packet instructions.

6. Remove the rosemary sprig and bay leaf from the lentil sauce and discard. Drain the cooked spaghetti and serve with the hot sauce, either tossing the sauce with the spaghetti or spooning it on top. Accompany with bread and a bowl of grated Parmesan to scatter over.

CHILLI CHICKEN WITH RAINBOW SLAW & KOREAN-STYLE GRAINS

This rainbow slaw can be eaten on its own when you want something quick and easy, or you can serve it as an accompaniment to grilled chicken or tofu skewers for a more substantial meal.

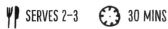 SERVES 2–3   30 MINS

INGREDIENTS

For the chilli chicken
- 150g chicken breast or thigh meat, skinless and boneless
- 1 tbsp gochujang (Korean chilli paste)
- 2 tbsp natural yoghurt
- finely grated zest of ½ lime

For the rainbow slaw
- ¼ red cabbage, any tough stalk removed
- ¼ white cabbage, any tough stalk removed
- 2 carrots, peeled
- 3 radishes
- 1 tbsp peeled and grated root ginger
- 2 tbsp apple cider vinegar
- 1 tsp gochujang (Korean chilli paste)
- 2 tbsp toasted sesame oil
- finely grated zest of ½ lime
- juice of 1 lime
- 25g unsalted peanuts
- 25g fresh coriander
- 1 red chilli, sliced
- 1 x 250g pouch of ready cooked Zingy Korean-style Grains

METHOD

1. To make the chilli chicken, cut the chicken into 2.5cm cubes. In a bowl, mix together the gochujang, yoghurt and lime zest. Add the chicken, stirring until the cubes are coated in the yoghurt mixture. Leave to marinate while you make the slaw.

2. To make the rainbow slaw, thinly slice the red and white cabbages, the carrots and radishes on a mandoline or use the slicing side of a grater. Put the sliced vegetables in a bowl, cover with cold water to keep them crisp and set aside.

3. Put the grated ginger into a small bowl and stir in the vinegar, gochujang, sesame oil and lime zest and juice. Roughly chop the peanuts and coriander and add to the cabbage mixture with the sliced chilli.

4. Pour three-quarters of the ginger and gochujang dressing over the rainbow slaw and toss everything together with your hands. Reserve the remaining dressing.

5. To cook the chilli chicken, thread the chicken cubes onto skewers. Heat a griddle pan until hot and place the skewers side by side on it. Cook for 5–10 minutes, turning the skewers occasionally, until the chicken is golden and cooked through.

6. Serve the skewers accompanied by the Korean-style grains, rainbow slaw and the reserved dressing poured over.

To make this vegetarian: replace the chicken with firm tofu.

To make this vegan: replace the chicken with firm tofu, and use dairy-free yoghurt.

CHICKEN, FREEKEH, HERB & SPRING VEGETABLE CASSEROLE

The vegetables added to this one-pot casserole can be varied according to the season and whichever vegetables are at their best. Spring vegetables are used here but, during the winter months, root vegetables such as parsnip, swede and main crop carrots would be equally good. You will need a large casserole with a lid that is suitable for both the hob and the oven and, depending on the vegetables used, you may need to vary the cooking time.

  SERVES 4   45 MINS

INGREDIENTS

- 2 tbsp olive oil
- 4 chicken drumsticks, skin on
- 4 chicken thighs, skin on
- 1 onion
- 2 cloves of garlic
- 2 celery sticks
- 6 baby carrots
- 500ml hot chicken stock
- 1 lemon
- 1 x 250g pouch of ready cooked Freekeh
- 100g asparagus spears
- 40g fresh or frozen peas
- 40g fresh or frozen broad beans
- 25g fresh tarragon
- 15g fresh flat-leaf parsley
- salt and black pepper

METHOD

1. Preheat the oven to 170°C (150°C fan)/Gas mark 3.

2. Heat the olive oil in a large flameproof casserole over a medium heat and brown the chicken pieces until golden all over. Season and remove them from the pan to a plate.

3. Peel and slice the onion and garlic, add them to the casserole and fry for about 3 minutes, stirring occasionally until softened.

4. Slice the celery, halve the carrots lengthways and add both to the pan. Cook for 1 minute, then return the chicken pieces to the pan.

5. Pour in the stock. Cut the lemon in half, squeeze in the juice and add the lemon halves as well. Stir in the freekeh, cover the casserole with a lid and cook in the oven for 30 minutes.

6. Cut the asparagus spears in half lengthways. Pod the peas and broad beans, if using fresh, or defrost if frozen. Remove any coarse stalks from the tarragon and parsley and chop the leaves.

7. Check to see if the chicken is cooked and, if so, add the asparagus, peas and broad beans and half the herbs. Replace the casserole lid and return it to the oven for a further 6–8 minutes.

8. Serve the casserole in wide, shallow bowls, sprinkled with the remaining herbs.

CHESTNUT TAGLIATELLE WITH SQUASH, SAGE & GOAT'S CHEESE

Finely ground roasted chestnuts are added to this pasta dough, making it light and nutty. If you don't have a pasta machine, buy ready-made tagliatelle, skip the pasta-making instructions and cook according to the packet instructions.

SERVES 4 · **50 MINS** · **(V) VEGETARIAN**

INGREDIENTS

For the chestnut tagliatelle
- ½ x 180g pouch of ready roasted Whole Chestnuts
- 300g '00' pasta flour, plus extra for dusting
- 3 free-range eggs
- 1 free-range egg yolk
- 1 tbsp olive oil

For the sauce
- 200g butternut squash, peeled, deseeded and cubed
- 2–3 tbsp olive oil, plus extra for drizzling
- 10 fresh sage leaves, finely chopped
- ½ x 180g pouch of ready roasted Whole Chestnuts
- 25g butter
- 50g soft goat's cheese, broken into small pieces
- salt and black pepper

METHOD

1. To make the chestnut tagliatelle, put the chestnuts in the bowl of a food processor and blitz to fine crumbs. Add the flour, eggs, egg yolk and olive oil and pulse until the mixture is crumbly. It should be soft enough to pinch together into a dough, so add a splash of cold water if it is too dry. Tip onto a lightly floured work surface and knead until smooth. Shape into a ball, wrap in cling film and refrigerate until needed.

2. Preheat the oven to 200°C (180°C fan)/Gas mark 6.

3. To make the sauce, toss the butternut squash cubes in the olive oil and season with salt, pepper and a good pinch of the chopped sage leaves, reserving the rest. Spread out the squash in a roasting tin and roast for 10–15 minutes or until tender and caramelized.

4. Cut the pasta dough into 4 pieces. Dust a work surface with flour and roll each piece of dough through a pasta machine into long strips, making the strips thinner each time you roll them, to a setting of 6, which should be a good thickness for tagliatelle. Once the strips are the right thickness, either put them through the machine again with the tagliatelle attachment fitted or roll up each strip and, using a sharp knife, cut into ½cm slices.

5. Roughly chop the chestnuts for the sauce and mix with the reserved sage. Melt the butter in a large frying pan over a low heat, add the chestnuts and sage and then the roasted squash.

6. Bring a large saucepan of lightly salted water to the boil and cook the pasta for 4–5 minutes.

7. Drain the pasta and tip it into the squash mixture in the pan. Stir, top with the goat's cheese and drizzle with olive oil.

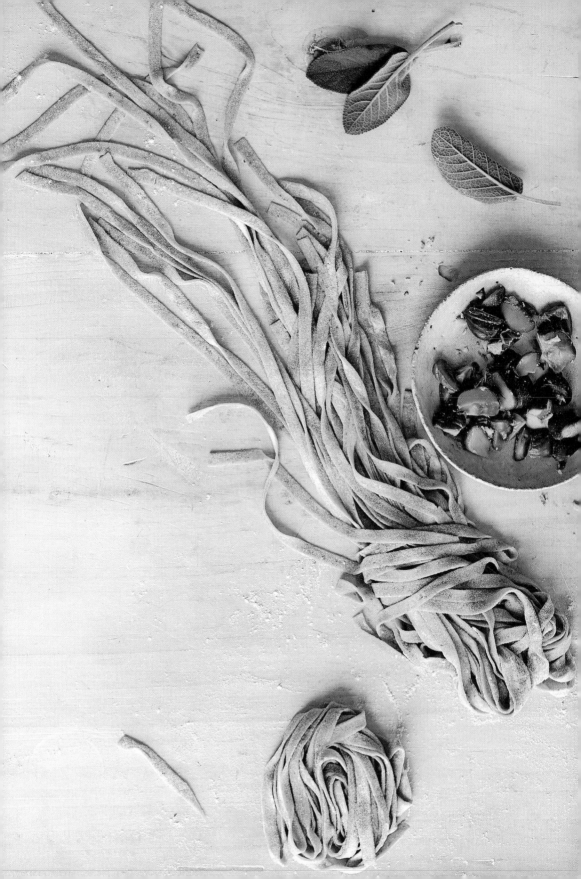

WILD MUSHROOMS & TRUFFLED LENTILS ON TOAST

When you feel like spoiling yourself on a weekday night but don't want
to spend ages in the kitchen, these wild mushrooms fried with garlic and
served on toast with truffled lentils are just what you need. For the ultimate
indulgence, drizzle the mushrooms with extra truffle-infused oil or even a few
shavings of fresh truffle.

 SERVES 2   10 MINS   (V) VEGETARIAN

INGREDIENTS
- 600g mixed wild mushrooms
- 25g fresh flat-leaf parsley
- 2 sprigs of fresh thyme
- 4 slices of sourdough bread
- 2 cloves of garlic, peeled
- 2 tbsp extra virgin olive oil
- 1 tbsp butter
- 1 x 250g pouch of ready
  cooked Puglian Lentils with
  Truffle Infused Oil
- 60ml double cream
- salt and black pepper

To serve (optional)
- fresh garlic chives
- truffle infused oil
- shavings of fresh truffle

METHOD
1. Rinse the mushrooms under cold water, brushing to remove
any soil sticking to them. Break any large mushrooms into
smaller pieces.

2. Roughly chop the parsley and pull the leaves off the
thyme sprigs.

3. Heat a ridged grill pan and toast the bread slices until they
are marked with attractive scorch lines. Rub the slices with
1 garlic clove and finely slice the other clove. Keep warm
while you cook the mushrooms.

4. Heat the olive oil in a large frying pan. Fry the sliced garlic
clove and mushrooms over a brisk heat so any liquid the
mushrooms release evaporates and they fry to a lovely golden
colour. Season with salt and plenty of black pepper. Add the
butter and lentils and stir everything together until combined.

5. Finally, stir in the cream, parsley and thyme leaves and cook
for 1–2 minutes until the cream has reduced and thickened.

6. Serve the mushrooms and lentils immediately, spooned
over the hot toast and sprinkled with garlic chives, drizzled
with truffle infused oil or topped with shavings of fresh truffle,
if wished.

To make this vegan: omit the butter and use a dairy-free cream.

QUINOA-CRUSTED CHICKEN KIEVS WITH ROASTED NEW POTATOES & BROCCOLI

Instead of using ordinary breadcrumbs, we've coated the chicken for this popular dish in red and white quinoa to give it a colourful and delicious twist. The cooked chicken is beautifully tender and oozes aromatic garlic butter.

 SERVES 2 1.5 HRS

INGREDIENTS
- 1 x 250g pouch of ready cooked Red & White Quinoa
- 200g new potatoes
- olive oil, for drizzling and frying
- 3 cloves of garlic
- 25g fresh flat-leaf parsley
- 75g butter, softened
- 2 chicken breasts, skinless and boneless
- 2 tbsp plain flour
- 1 free-range egg
- 175g Tenderstem broccoli
- salt and black pepper

METHOD

1. Preheat the oven to 200°C (180°C fan)/Gas mark 6.

2. Spread the quinoa evenly on a baking tray and roast for 15 minutes until it is dry and crisp. Leave the oven on.

3. Halve the potatoes and cook them in a pan of lightly salted, boiling water for 5 minutes. Drain and drizzle with olive oil, and season with salt and pepper. Bruise 1 of the cloves of garlic and add to the potatoes. Spread out in a baking tray and roast for about 25 minutes or until golden and crisp.

4. Meanwhile, using a food processor or pestle and mortar, pound the remaining garlic, the parsley and butter to a paste. Season with salt and pepper.

5. Lay the chicken breasts on a board and, using a sharp knife, cut a deep pocket in each, starting at the thicker end. Stuff each pocket with one-third of the flavoured butter (reserve the last third). Reshape the chicken breasts so the butter is enclosed and seal each pocket with a cocktail stick. Refrigerate for 30 minutes.

6. Spread the flour on a large plate, beat the egg in a shallow dish and spread the quinoa on another large plate. Dredge the chicken in the flour, coat all over with beaten egg, then press them into the quinoa, making sure it is evenly coated.

7. Line a baking tray with foil. Put the chicken on the tray and fold the foil over at the edges to catch any escaping butter. Bake in the oven for 25 minutes, or until cooked through.

8. Steam the broccoli until it is just tender. Drain and stir the remaining butter through the broccoli and potatoes to coat. Serve with the chicken Kievs.

COURGETTE, LENTIL & PARMESAN FRITTERS WITH COURGETTE SALAD

These crisp fritters are a cross between a falafel and a vegetarian version of *polpette*, the Italian meatballs made with minced veal or beef. Serve them stuffed into pitta breads with vegetable pickles.

 SERVES 3–4   20 MINS   VEGETARIAN

INGREDIENTS

For the courgette, lentil & Parmesan fritters
- 1 courgette
- 75g (vegetarian-friendly) Parmesan cheese, grated
- 2 lemons
- 25g fresh mint leaves
- 2 spring onions, trimmed
- 1 x 250g pouch of ready cooked Champagne Lentils
- 5 tbsp gram/chickpea flour
- 100ml vegetable oil
- salt and black pepper

For the courgette salad
- 4 tbsp olive oil
- ½ tsp mustard
- 2 courgettes
- 6 radishes
- a handful of fresh mint leaves
- a handful of fresh basil leaves

To serve
- natural yoghurt
- pitta breads
- vegetable pickles

METHOD

1. To make the courgette, lentil & Parmesan fritters, grate the courgette into a large bowl and add the Parmesan. Grate in the zest from the lemons and squeeze in the juice from 1 lemon, reserving the juice from the other lemon for the salad dressing.

2. Thinly slice the mint leaves and spring onions and add to the bowl with the lentils. Stir in the gram flour and season with salt and pepper, mixing everything together. If the mixture is a little dry, add a splash of water and stir again until it can be shaped into 12 patties.

3. Heat the oil in a frying pan over medium heat and fry the patties for about 5 minutes on each side until they are golden brown, turning them over carefully.

4. To make the dressing for the courgette salad, whisk together the olive oil, reserved juice from the remaining lemon, and the mustard. Season with salt and pepper.

5. Shave the courgettes into thin ribbons using a vegetable peeler, cut the radishes into thin slivers and place both on a large serving platter. Remove any tough stalks from the herbs and tear the leaves over the courgettes and radishes. Pour over the dressing and toss everything together.

6. Serve the salad with the fritters and accompany with natural yoghurt to spoon over, pitta breads and vegetable pickles.

KOREAN BIBIMBAP BOWL WITH CHILLI BEEF & FRIED EGG

Bibimbap is a Korean dish, the word literally translating as 'rice bowl'. The dish is a great way to use Korean-style grains, and in this recipe they're served with chilli beef, quick mixed pickles, vegetables, prawn crackers and – as is traditional in Korea – a fried egg on top.

 SERVES 2 20 MINS

INGREDIENTS

For the vegetable pickles
- 3 radishes
- ⅓ cucumber
- 1 carrot
- 120ml rice wine vinegar
- ½ tsp salt
- 1 tbsp caster sugar

For the chilli beef
- 2 tbsp light olive oil
- 220g lean minced beef
- 2 cloves of garlic, peeled and finely chopped
- ½ chilli, finely chopped
- 1 tbsp gochujang (Korean chilli paste), plus extra to serve
- 1 x 250g pouch of ready cooked Zingy Korean-style Grains

For the toppings
- 2 free-range eggs
- 1 tbsp light olive oil
- ½ red pepper, deseeded and sliced
- 90g edamame beans
- 50g beansprouts
- prawn crackers

METHOD

1. To make the vegetable pickles, quarter the radishes, slice the cucumber, and peel and shave the carrot into ribbons using a vegetable peeler. Set aside in a bowl. Heat the vinegar, 80ml water, and the salt and sugar in a pan until the sugar dissolves. Bring to the boil, then pour over the prepared vegetables. Leave to cool.

2. To make the chilli beef, heat the oil in a large frying pan, add the minced beef and fry for 3–4 minutes until the beef starts to brown. Add the garlic, chilli and gochujang and cook for a further 5 minutes. Push the mixture to one side of the pan, add the Korean-style grains to the other side and warm it through for 3 minutes.

3. For the toppings, in another frying pan, fry the eggs in the oil until the whites are set and crisp around the edges.

4. Divide the hot Korean-style grains between 2 shallow serving bowls, add the red pepper slices, drained vegetable pickles, beef chilli, edamame beans and beansprouts. Top each bowl with a fried egg and serve with extra gochujang and prawn crackers.

PORK & CHILLI MEATBALLS WITH TOMATO SAUCE & SPANISH-STYLE GRAINS & RICE

These herby meatballs, made with lean minced pork and spiked with hot chilli, are baked in a rich tomato sauce and topped with cheese. You can prepare the dish ahead, ready to go into the oven, so all you have left to do is to heat up the Spanish-style grains & rice. If you don't have a frying pan that can be used in the oven, transfer the cooked meatballs in tomato sauce to a shallow baking dish and bake them in that instead.

  **SERVES 4** **40 MINS**

INGREDIENTS

- 400g lean minced pork
- ½ red onion, peeled and finely chopped
- 1 clove of garlic, peeled and grated or finely chopped
- 15g fresh flat-leaf parsley, finely chopped
- 1 jalapeño chilli, deseeded and finely chopped
- 55g fresh breadcrumbs
- a pinch of dried chilli flakes
- 1 free-range egg, beaten
- 1 tbsp olive oil
- 1 x 400g can of chopped tomatoes
- 100g Cheddar cheese, grated

To serve
- 1 x 250g pouch of ready cooked Smoky Spanish-style Grains & Rice
- finely chopped fresh flat-leaf parsley

METHOD

1. In a large bowl, mix together the minced pork, red onion, garlic, parsley, chopped chilli, breadcrumbs and chilli flakes. Stir in the beaten egg, then knead with your hands until the mixture comes together. If you prefer, you can do this in a food processor, but take care not to over-process the ingredients or the minced pork will lose its texture and become a mush.

2. With lightly oiled or dampened hands, roll the mixture into 12 evenly sized balls.

3. Preheat the oven to 200°C (180°C fan)/Gas mark 6.

4. Heat the olive oil in a large, ovenproof frying pan and fry the meatballs until they are browned all over, turning them carefully from time to time so they colour and cook evenly. Add the chopped tomatoes, fill the can with cold water and add this to the frying pan as well.

5. Transfer the pan to the oven and bake for 20 minutes. Stir the sauce, sprinkle the grated cheese over the top and bake for a further 5 minutes.

6. To serve, heat the Spanish-style grains & rice in a saucepan and serve with the meatballs. Garnish with chopped parsley sprinkled over.

Weekend
Feasts

RICH TOMATO, BAY LEAF & LENTIL LASAGNE

This is a quick and easy lasagne, using vegetable Bolognese in a different way. Here it is layered up with sheets of fresh pasta and a cheesy béchamel sauce infused with bay leaves.

 SERVES 4   35 MINS   VEGETARIAN

INGREDIENTS
- 300ml milk
- 2 bay leaves
- 3 tbsp butter
- 3 tbsp plain flour
- 1 quantity of Tomatoey Lentil Bolognese (see page 92)
- 6 sheets of fresh lasagne
- 60g (vegetarian-friendly) Cheddar cheese, grated
- 20g (vegetarian-friendly) Parmesan cheese, grated
- black pepper
- rocket salad, to serve

METHOD
1. Preheat the oven to 190°C (170°C fan)/Gas mark 5.

2. To make a béchamel sauce, heat the milk and bay leaves in a saucepan until bubbles appear on the surface. Remove from the heat and leave the milk to infuse for 5 minutes. Strain the milk into a bowl or jug and discard the bay leaves.

3. Rinse out the pan, add the butter to it and, when melted, take the pan off the heat and stir in the flour until smooth. Return the pan to the heat and cook for about 2 minutes. Take the pan off the heat again and slowly stir or whisk in the milk so there are no lumps.

4. Return the pan to the heat and stir constantly until the béchamel sauce is thickened and smooth. Season with freshly ground black pepper.

5. In a shallow ovenproof dish, layer up the Lentil Bolognese, béchamel sauce and lasagne sheets (trimming the sheets with scissors to fit into the dish, if necessary). Repeat the layers until the ingredients are used up (about 4 layers) finishing with a layer of the sauce.

6. Sprinkle over the grated Cheddar and Parmesan cheeses and bake in the oven for 15–20 minutes until the top is golden and bubbling.

7. Serve with a simple salad of dressed rocket.

CUMIN-SPICED CARROT & LENTIL BURGERS WITH SPICY MAYONNAISE

Shape the lentil mixture into 4 spicy burgers or, if you prefer, 8–10 mini burgers called sliders. Topped with avocado, rocket, red onion and spicy mayonnaise, this is without doubt fast food at its fastest and very best.

 SERVES 4   25 MINS   VEGETARIAN

INGREDIENTS

For the cumin-spiced carrot & lentil burgers
- 1 x 250g pouch of ready cooked Beluga® Lentils
- 2 tbsp cumin seeds
- 1 tsp ground turmeric
- 1 tsp dried chilli flakes
- 4 tbsp gram/chickpea flour
- 2 large carrots (total weight about 120g)
- 2 spring onions, trimmed
- 2 tbsp olive oil
- salt and black pepper

For the spicy mayonnaise
- 1 tsp sriracha sauce
- 4 tbsp mayonnaise

To serve
- brioche buns, cut in half
- rocket
- avocado slices
- red onion slices

METHOD

1. To make the cumin-spiced carrot & lentil burgers, mix the lentils, cumin seeds, turmeric, chilli flakes and gram flour together in a large bowl. Season with salt and pepper.

2. Coarsely grate the carrots and slice the spring onions.

3. Add the carrots and half the sliced onions to the lentil mixture. Using your hands (wear thin disposable gloves, if you prefer), work the ingredients together and then shape into patties to make 4 burgers or 8–10 sliders.

4. Heat a large frying pan over a medium heat, add the olive oil and, when hot, fry the patties for 4–6 minutes on each side until evenly golden. They should be crisp on the outside but soft in the middle. Keep warm in a low oven while you layer up each burger.

5. To make the spicy mayonnaise, stir the sriracha sauce into the mayonnaise.

6. To serve, spread the cut sides of the buns with the spicy mayonnaise, add a layer of rocket followed by a burger, some avocado slices, the remaining spring onion slices, red onion slices and finish with another spoonful of mayonnaise.

7. Serve on their own or with sweet potato fries and more of the spicy mayonnaise.

To make this vegan: use vegan-friendly buns and mayonnaise.

LENTIL CHILI WITH CHARRED CORN, AVOCADO & TOMATO SALSA, & TORTILLAS

Chocolate is the secret ingredient in this chili. It might sound odd but a little chocolate – don't be tempted to add too much – gives the chili a marvellous depth of flavour. Serve in a large pot surrounded by the accompaniments.

 SERVES 4    30 MINS   VEGETARIAN

INGREDIENTS

For the lentil chili
- 1 red onion
- 1 carrot
- 1 leek
- 2 cloves of garlic
- 2 tbsp olive oil
- 1 tsp ground cumin
- 2 bay leaves
- 3 dried chillies, finely chopped and seeds removed, if preferred
- 1 tsp paprika
- 1 tbsp dried oregano
- 1 tbsp cocoa powder
- 2 tbsp tomato purée
- 1 x 400g can of chopped tomatoes
- 1 x 250g pouch of ready cooked Puy Lentils
- 1 x 400g can of kidney beans, drained and rinsed
- 25g dark chocolate, chopped
- salt and black pepper

For the accompaniments
- 2 corn on the cobs
- 1 avocado
- 1 jalapeño chilli
- 1 plum tomato
- 150ml sour cream
- 2 limes
- 15g fresh coriander, chopped
- tortilla chips

METHOD

1. To make the lentil chili, peel and finely dice the onion and carrot. Trim and thinly slice the leek and peel and crush the garlic. Heat the oil in a large pan over a medium heat and sweat the vegetables until they are softened.

2. Add the cumin, bay leaves, chillies, paprika, oregano and cocoa powder and cook for 2 minutes to release their flavour.

3. Stir in the tomato purée and cook for 1 minute. Add the chopped tomatoes, fill the can with water and tip this into the pan as well. Simmer for 5 minutes, then add the lentils and kidney beans.

4. Season and cook for 15 minutes until the sauce begins to thicken. Just before serving, stir in the chopped chocolate so that it melts into the sauce.

5. For the accompaniments, place a griddle pan or frying pan over a high heat and place the corn cobs in it. Cook and turn until the corn is nicely charred.

6. Halve the avocado, remove the stone and scoop out the flesh. Mash until smooth. Finely dice the jalapeño chilli and chop the tomato and mix both with the avocado. Stir in a tablespoon of the sour cream and a squeeze of lime. Season.

7. Put the avocado and tomato salsa, the remaining sour cream mixed with the coriander, and the remaining lime cut into wedges, into separate bowls and serve with the chili and corn, plus some tortilla chips.

To make this vegan: use vegan dark chocolate and a dairy-free alternative to sour cream.

CHICKEN DHANSAK WITH HOMEMADE RAITA

Dhansak is a spicy curry traditionally made with lentils and vegetables, plus a meat such as chicken or lamb. It has a hot, tangy flavour that is balanced by stirring fresh tomatoes and spinach into the sauce at the end of cooking.

 SERVES 4 50 MINS

INGREDIENTS

For the chicken dhansak
- 100g dried Puy Lentils
- 2 white onions
- 2 cloves of garlic
- 2.5cm piece of root ginger
- 2 tbsp coconut oil
- 3 chicken breasts, skinless, boneless and cut into bite-size pieces
- 1 tsp ground cumin
- 1 tsp ground turmeric
- 1 tsp ground coriander
- 1 tsp dried chilli flakes
- 1 tsp fenugreek
- 1 small piece of cassia bark or cinnamon stick
- 1 tbsp brown sugar
- 2 tsp white wine vinegar
- 1 x 400g can of chopped tomatoes
- 500ml hot chicken stock
- 2 large tomatoes
- 100g baby spinach leaves

For the homemade raita
- ½ cucumber
- 200ml natural Greek yoghurt
- 1 tsp dried mint

To serve
- fresh coriander leaves
- papadums
- Indian chutneys and pickles

METHOD

1. To make the dhansak, rinse the lentils.

2. Peel and roughly chop the onions, garlic and ginger. Grind to a paste in a food processor (or finely chop with a sharp knife).

3. Heat 1 tablespoon of the coconut oil in a large saucepan and seal the chicken pieces in the hot oil in batches, removing them to a plate as they brown.

4. Add the remaining oil to the pan with the cumin, turmeric, ground coriander, chilli flakes, fenugreek and cassia bark or cinnamon stick and fry, stirring constantly, for 2 minutes. Stir in the onion paste and cook for 5 minutes before adding the brown sugar and vinegar.

5. Stir in the lentils and return the chicken to the pan. Add the can of chopped tomatoes and the stock. Reduce the heat, cover the pan with a lid and cook the dhansak over a low heat for 30–40 minutes until the lentils start to break down and thicken the sauce. Stir occasionally to stop the sauce sticking to the bottom of the pan.

6. Roughly chop the tomatoes and, 5 minutes before serving, stir in, along with the spinach.

7. To make the homemade raita, grate the cucumber into a small bowl and stir in the yoghurt and mint.

8. To serve, remove the cassia bark or cinnamon stick and discard. Sprinkle the dhansak with coriander leaves and accompany with the raita, papadums and Indian chutneys and pickles.

LAMB CHOPS WITH MINT & POMEGRANATE COUSCOUS & PISTACHIO PESTO

A delicious feast of succulent lamb chops served with a mint and pistachio pesto and a jewelled pomegranate and lemon salad made with wholewheat giant couscous. Racks of lamb that you carve into cutlets at the table will make any occasion special or you can grill individual chops, if you prefer. You can prepare the couscous ahead of time and just cook the lamb when you need it.

 SERVES 4 40 MINS

INGREDIENTS

For the lamb chops
- 1 rack of lamb
  (or 8 individual lamb chops)
- 2 tbsp olive oil
- salt and black pepper

For the mint & pomegranate couscous
- 2 tbsp olive oil
- 300g dried Wholewheat
  Giant Couscous
- finely grated zest and juice
  of 2 lemons
- 2 tbsp pomegranate molasses
- 25g fresh mint, leaves picked
  from their stalks
- seeds from 1 pomegranate
- 40g sultanas

For the pistachio pesto
- 50g shelled pistachios
- 10g fresh mint leaves
- 1 clove of garlic
- 3 tbsp olive oil
- 1 tbsp lemon juice

METHOD

1. To cook the lamb, preheat the oven to 220°C (200°C fan)/ Gas mark 7.

2. Heat a large frying pan. Season the rack of lamb and rub the olive oil over it. Brown it all over in the hot pan, then transfer to a roasting tin. Roast in the oven for 8–12 minutes until the internal temperature of the meat reaches 54°C for pink lamb, or a little longer if you want it well done. Remove from the oven and leave the lamb in the tin, covered in foil, to rest.

3. To make the mint & pomegranate couscous, heat the olive oil in a saucepan, add the couscous and toast it for 1 minute. Pour in 400ml water, bring to the boil and simmer for 15 minutes or until the couscous has absorbed the water and the grains are tender. Leave to cool.

4. Mix the lemon juice and molasses together, season and add to the couscous. Finely chop the mint leaves and add to the couscous with the lemon zest, pomegranate seeds and sultanas.

5. To make the pistachio pesto, blend all the ingredients together or crush with a pestle and mortar to make a chunky paste.

6. Check the lamb and reheat it briefly in the oven. Carve into individual cutlets and serve with the couscous and the pesto on top.

LENTIL COTTAGE PIE WITH CHEESY MASHED POTATO

Here is a vegetarian alternative to a family favourite. The pie is made with dried Puy lentils that retain their shape when cooked and add a lovely peppery flavour. And the creamy mash and melting cheese are great comfort food.

 SERVES 4–6   1 HR   VEGETARIAN

INGREDIENTS
- 1 onion
- 2 cloves of garlic
- 1 carrot
- 1 leek
- 1 celery stick
- 2 tbsp olive oil
- 1 tbsp fresh thyme leaves, chopped
- 1 tbsp fresh rosemary leaves, chopped
- 1 tbsp garam masala
- 250g dried Puy Lentils
- 1 x 400g can of chopped tomatoes
- 2 tbsp tomato purée
- 2 tbsp vegetable gravy granules
- 500ml hot vegetable stock
- 100g frozen peas
- salt and black pepper

For the mashed potato topping
- 700g Maris Piper potatoes (or another variety suitable for mashing)
- 100ml milk
- 35g butter, diced
- 4 spring onions, trimmed and thinly sliced
- 50g (vegetarian-friendly) Cheddar cheese, grated

METHOD
1. Peel the onion, garlic and carrot and cut into small dice. Trim the leek and celery and cut into evenly sized dice. Heat the oil in a saucepan, add the vegetables and sweat them for 5 minutes until softened. Add the thyme, rosemary, garam masala and lentils and cook for 2 minutes.

2. Add the tomatoes, tomato purée, gravy granules and stock, stir well and bring to a simmer. Cook for 15–20 minutes or until the lentils are just soft. Stir in the peas, season and spoon into a pie dish. Set aside to cool.

3. Meanwhile, to make the mashed potato topping, peel and cut the potatoes into evenly sized chunks. Boil in a pan of salted water for 10–15 minutes until tender. Drain, return to the saucepan and mash. Push the potatoes to one side of the pan, add the milk to the other side and heat the milk before mixing it into the potatoes – warming the milk makes the mash extra light and fluffy. Stir in the butter and sliced spring onions.

4. Preheat the oven to 200°C (180°C fan)/Gas mark 6.

5. Spoon the mashed potatoes on top of the lentil mixture, swirling the potatoes into peaks with a fork so they crisp up in the oven. Sprinkle with the grated cheese and bake in the oven for 25–30 minutes until golden. Serve with vegetables or a green salad.

BEEF & LENTIL MASSAMAN CURRY WITH BABY POTATOES & GREEN BEANS

This rich, slow-cooked beef curry is relatively mild for a Thai dish. It is infused with many of that country's aromatic flavours, such as coconut, lemon grass and peanut. Adding lentils and potatoes turns it into a robust one-pot dish. If you have a slow cooker, put everything into the pot, adding the potatoes and lentils towards the end.

 SERVES 4   2.5 HRS

INGREDIENTS
- 2 tbsp coconut oil
- 400g braising steak, cubed
- 2 shallots
- 2 cloves of garlic
- 1 lemon grass stalk
- 2 dried bird's eye chillies
- 2 whole star anise
- 2 tbsp massaman curry paste
- 2 x 400g cans of coconut milk
- 100g baby potatoes
- 1 x 250g pouch of ready cooked Puy Lentils
- 100g green beans
- 25g unsalted peanuts, chopped
- fresh coriander leaves, to serve

METHOD
1. Preheat the oven to 190°C (170°C fan)/Gas mark 5.

2. Heat the coconut oil in a large flameproof casserole and brown the steak in batches.

3. While the beef is browning, peel and finely slice the shallots and garlic. Add them to the casserole with the beef, crush the lemon grass stalk to release its flavour and add this as well, along with the chillies and star anise. Cook for 5 minutes or until the shallots have softened.

4. Stir in the curry paste and coconut milk and bring to the boil. Cover the casserole with a lid and cook in the oven for 1 hour 45 minutes, stirring occasionally, until the meat is almost tender.

5. Wash the potatoes and cut them in half. Add them to the curry and return the casserole to the oven for 20 minutes before stirring in the lentils.

6. Blanch the green beans in a saucepan of lightly salted boiling water for 5 minutes. Drain and stir into the curry.

7. Serve the curry with the chopped peanuts and the coriander leaves sprinkled over.

VENISON, CHESTNUT, MUSHROOM & RED WINE PIE

Venison meat cut from the leg and slowly stewed makes a rich and warming filling for this pie. What's great is that the pie can be made ahead (ensure the meat mixture is cold before you add the pastry lid) and baked later.

 SERVES 4   3 HRS

INGREDIENTS
- 15g dried porcini mushrooms
- 2 tbsp olive oil
- 2 onions, thinly sliced
- 3 cloves of garlic, thinly sliced
- 600g venison leg meat, cut into 2cm dice
- 1 tbsp plain flour, plus extra for rolling out the pastry
- 3 juniper berries, crushed
- 1 bay leaf
- sprig of fresh rosemary
- 300ml red wine
- 1 x 180g pouch of ready roasted Whole Chestnuts
- 600ml hot beef or game stock
- 1 x 500g block of puff pastry
- 1 free-range egg yolk
- 1 tbsp milk
- salt and black pepper

METHOD
1. Soak the dried porcini in 200ml boiling water while you continue with the recipe.

2. Preheat the oven to 200°C (180°C fan)/Gas mark 6.

3. Heat 1 tablespoon of the olive oil in a flameproof casserole over a medium heat and sweat the onions and garlic until softened. Remove them from the pan to a plate and set aside. Add the remaining olive oil to the casserole.

4. Season the venison with salt and pepper and toss in the flour until evenly coated. Fry the diced meat until browned all over, then return the onions and garlic to the casserole and add the juniper berries, bay leaf and rosemary.

5. Pour in the wine, bubble for 5 minutes until reduced and then add the porcini and their soaking liquid, the chestnuts and stock. Give everything a good stir – there will be a lot of liquid – and cover with a lid. Cook in the oven for 30 minutes.

6. Lower the oven to 180°C (160°C fan)/Gas mark 4 and cook for a further 2 hours or until the meat is so tender it is falling apart. If the liquid has reduced too much, add a little water.

7. Remove the rosemary, spoon the meat into a 20cm pie dish, 5cm deep, and leave to cool while you roll out the pastry. Turn the oven back up to 200°C (180°C fan)/Gas mark 6.

8. Roll out the pastry on a floured surface and lift it over the pie filling. Trim and pinch the edges with your fingers. Beat the egg yolk with the milk and brush over the pastry to glaze.

9. Bake the pie for 20 minutes or until the pastry has puffed up and is crisp and golden brown. Serve accompanied by creamy mashed potatoes – and, of course, a glass of good red wine!

STICKY SLOW-COOKED PORK SHOULDER WITH GARLIC GREENS & KOREAN-STYLE GRAINS

Slow-cooking a pork joint in the oven for several hours makes the meat so meltingly tender it simply falls off the bone. Served with greens tossed with garlic and sesame oil, and spicy Korean-style grains, it's a dish that would make a superb centrepiece for a feast to share with friends.

 SERVES 4   5 HRS

INGREDIENTS

For the sticky slow-cooked pork
- 2kg joint of shoulder of pork, on the bone
- 3 tbsp olive oil
- 2 tbsp gochujang (Korean chilli paste)
- 1 tbsp smoked paprika
- 1 tsp salt
- 1 tsp black pepper

For the garlic greens
- 2 tbsp toasted sesame oil
- 400g mixed greens (e.g. kale, cavolo nero, green cabbage), torn
- 3 cloves of garlic, peeled and thinly sliced
- 1 x 250g pouch of ready cooked Zingy Korean-style Grains
- juice of ½ lemon

METHOD

1. To cook the pork, preheat the oven to 220°C (200°C fan)/Gas mark 7.

2. Lift the pork joint into a large roasting tin. Rub it all over with the olive oil followed by the gochujang and the smoked paprika. Season with the salt and pepper.

3. Roast the pork in the oven for 30 minutes. Pour 500ml of cold water into the roasting tin, cover tightly with baking parchment and foil and lower the oven temperature to 180°C (160°C fan)/Gas mark 4. Roast for a further 4 hours or until the meat is starting to pull away from the bone in shreds.

4. Pour off the cooking juices and reserve for later. Turn the oven back up to 220°C (200°C fan)/Gas mark 7 and remove the foil. Roast the pork for a further 15–20 minutes to crisp up the crackling. Pull the meat apart with 2 large forks.

5. To make the garlic greens, heat the sesame oil in a large frying pan, add the greens and garlic and cook for a couple of minutes until the garlic starts to turn golden. Heat the Korean-style grains following the pack instructions. Stir in the greens and garlic and squeeze over the lemon juice.

6. Serve the garlic greens and rice with the pulled pork and the cooking juices poured over.

BREADED FISH TACOS WITH AVOCADO CREAM, SLAW & CHIPOTLE MAYONNAISE

'Posh fish finger sandwiches' is how we'd describe these tacos. Put the crunchy fish, Mexican grains, red cabbage slaw, cooling avocado, spicy mayonnaise and other accompaniments in separate bowls so guests can build their own tacos.

 SERVES 4　 30 MINS

INGREDIENTS

For the fish goujons
- 300g white fish fillets, skinned and cut into 2cm strips
- 2 tbsp plain flour
- 2 free-range eggs, beaten
- 150g panko (dry breadcrumbs)
- 200ml vegetable oil for frying

For the slaw
- 1 red onion, thinly sliced
- ¼ red cabbage, thinly sliced
- 10g fresh coriander, chopped
- 2 tbsp red wine vinegar
- ½ tsp salt

For the avocado cream
- 1 avocado
- juice of 2 limes
- 4 tbsp sour cream
- salt and black pepper

For the chipotle mayonnaise
- 2 tbsp chipotle sauce
- 4 tbsp mayonnaise

To serve
- 1 x 250g pouch of ready cooked Spicy Mexican-style Grains & Pulses
- leaves from 1 baby gem lettuce
- 1 jalapeño chilli, thinly sliced
- 8 small corn tortillas
- sprigs of fresh coriander

METHOD

1. To make the fish goujons, coat the fish strips in flour, then in the beaten eggs and then in the breadcrumbs. Press the crumbs over the strips until evenly coated and shake off any excess. Put the breaded strips on a plate and refrigerate while you prepare the accompaniments.

2. To make the slaw, mix the sliced vegetables and coriander with the vinegar and salt.

3. To make the avocado cream, halve the avocado and remove the stone. Scoop out the flesh into a blender, add the lime juice and sour cream and blend until smooth. Season with salt and pepper.

4. To make the chipotle mayonnaise, stir the chipotle sauce into the mayonnaise.

5. To serve, put the slaw, avocado cream, chipotle mayonnaise, Mexican grains, lettuce and chilli into separate bowls and store in the fridge until needed.

6. Warm the tortillas in a hot pan and wrap in a tea towel to keep them hot.

7. Heat the vegetable oil in the same pan and fry the fish goujons until golden brown and crisp. Drain and place in a serving dish with the coriander sprigs as a garnish.

8. Serve the goujons with the bowls of accompaniments and warm tortillas, leaving everyone to help themselves and build their own tacos.

SPICY PAPRIKA PRAWNS WITH GARLIC, CHILLI & SPANISH-STYLE GRAINS & RICE

This irresistible combination of king prawns grilled with spicy butter and served over a salad of Spanish-style grains & rice, tossed with parsley and red pepper, makes a superb lunch dish. Whatever the weather outside, you'll imagine you're sitting at a beach-side café in the Mediterranean sunshine.

 SERVES 2–4   20 MINS

INGREDIENTS
- 40g butter, diced and softened
- 1 clove of garlic, peeled and grated or finely chopped
- 1 tsp smoked paprika
- 1 tsp dried chilli flakes
- 1 x 250g pouch of ready cooked Smoky Spanish-style Grains & Rice
- 2 tbsp chopped fresh flat-leaf parsley, plus extra to garnish
- 1 red pepper, deseeded and diced
- 500g fresh or frozen raw king prawns, unpeeled (defrosted if frozen)
- 1 lemon, cut into wedges, to serve

METHOD
1. Mash together the butter, garlic, smoked paprika and chilli flakes until combined.

2. Empty the Spanish rice into a bowl and stir in the chopped parsley and red pepper.

3. Heat a griddle pan until very hot. Add the prawns and cook for 2–4 minutes on each side, depending on size, until the prawns are golden and their flesh is opaque. Add the garlic and spiced butter to the griddle and toss the prawns in the melting butter until coated.

4. Spoon the rice mixture into a serving bowl. Drizzle any buttery juices from the pan over the rice and scatter over some chopped parsley. Serve with the hot prawns and lemon wedges.

BLACK BEAN, AVOCADO & RED PEPPER QUESADILLA STACKS WITH TOMATO SALSA

This is a variation on classic quesadillas that makes an unusual and very tasty vegan lunch or supper dish. Accompany with a beer that's suitable for vegans – served ice-cold, of course – and it will be a guaranteed crowd-pleaser.

 SERVES 4 20 MINS  VEGAN

INGREDIENTS

For the tomato salsa
- 1 beef tomato, diced
- 1 jalapeño chilli, diced
- 1 spring onion, trimmed and sliced
- 15g fresh coriander, chopped
- juice of 1 lime
- 1½ tbsp olive oil
- salt and black pepper

For the avocado & red pepper quesadillas
- 4 large corn tortilla wraps
- 1 x 250g pouch of ready cooked Smoky Spanish-style Grains & Rice
- 200g canned black beans, drained and rinsed
- 1 tsp nutritional yeast flakes
- 1 spring onion, trimmed and sliced
- 60g dairy-free hard cheese alternative, grated
- 1 avocado, halved, peeled, stoned and diced
- 100g flame-roasted red peppers from a jar, well drained and sliced

METHOD

1. To make the tomato salsa, mix all the ingredients together and season with salt and pepper.

2. To make the avocado & red pepper quesadillas, preheat the oven to 200°C (180°C fan)/Gas mark 6.

3. Lay 2 tortillas, side by side, on a board and divide the Spanish-style grains & rice and the black beans between them, spreading both right to the edge of the tortillas.

4. Sprinkle over the nutritional yeast, spring onion and grated cheese alternative, dividing them equally between the tortillas. Lay the diced avocado and pepper slices on top.

5. Add a tablespoon of the salsa to each and season to taste. Lay the remaining tortillas on top and press down lightly to keep them in place.

6. Heat a large frying pan and, when hot, use 2 fish slices to lift a quesadilla stack into the pan. Fry for 2 minutes on each side until crisp, carefully turning the stack over with the fish slices. Lift the stack out of the pan onto a baking tray and fry the second stack in the same way.

7. Place the quesadilla stacks in the oven for 5 minutes so the filling inside is hot and melted. Remove from the oven, cut each stack into 4 and serve at once with the remaining salsa on the side.

Sweet
Treats

CRANBERRY, QUINOA & SPELT COOKIES

These lovely red and white cookies are both chewy and crunchy, guaranteed to be a hit with all the family. The dough will keep in the fridge or freezer and then baked whenever you want fresh cookies – perfect for teatime.

 MAKES 12   45 MINS   (V) VEGETARIAN

INGREDIENTS
- 80g unsalted butter
- 30g golden syrup
- 75g caster sugar
- 30g jumbo oats
- 30g spelt flakes
- 1 x 250g pouch of ready cooked Red & White Quinoa
- 100g self-raising flour
- 100g dried cranberries
- 1 free-range egg
- ½ tsp vanilla paste or 1 tsp vanilla extract

METHOD
1. Preheat the oven to 180°C (160°C fan)/Gas mark 4. Line 2 baking trays with baking parchment.

2. Melt the butter and golden syrup together in a small saucepan.

3. In a bowl, mix together the sugar, oats, spelt flakes, quinoa, flour and cranberries and mix well.

4. Beat in the egg and vanilla and then add the melted butter mixture. Mix until well combined.

5. Put the bowl in the fridge and leave to firm up for 15 minutes.

6. Roll the mixture into 12 balls with your hands and divide between the baking trays, spacing them well apart so the cookies have room to spread. Flatten the balls slightly with your fingers or a fork.

7. Bake for about 15–20 minutes, or until just turning golden. Leave to firm up on the baking trays for about 5 minutes before transferring to a wire rack to cool.

MAPLE & LENTIL FUDGE BITES

These little treats make the perfect accompaniment to after-dinner coffee.
They have a soft, fudgy texture, similar to traditional chocolate truffles, but
are dairy-and gluten-free. One will never be enough!

 MAKES 25-30   20 MINS   (VE) VEGAN

INGREDIENTS

• 1 x 250g pouch of ready
  cooked Champagne Lentils
• 5 tbsp coconut oil
• 60g cocoa powder
• 5 tbsp maple syrup
• melted vegan chocolate
  or extra cocoa powder,
  for coating (optional)

METHOD

1. Grease and line a 20-cm square tin with baking parchment.

2. Tip the lentils into a food processor, add the coconut oil,
cocoa powder and maple syrup and blend until smooth.

3. Scrape the mixture out of the food processor into the tin
and press it down in an even layer with the back of a spoon.

4. Chill in the fridge for 10 minutes to set.

5. Turn out, peel off the lining paper and cut into squares.
Serve the bites plain or dip them in melted chocolate and
leave to set on a rack over a sheet of baking parchment to
catch any drips. Alternatively, roll them in cocoa powder until
coated on all sides. Store in the fridge until ready to serve.

DARK CHOCOLATE & CHESTNUT POTS

These rich chocolate pots would make a memorable dessert, turning any get-together into a special occasion. They can even be prepared a day ahead. Smooth and silky, they have a hint of creamy chestnut running through them.

 SERVES 4–6   2 HRS OR OVERNIGHT   VEGETARIAN

INGREDIENTS
- 3 free-range egg yolks
- 60g dark muscovado sugar
- 1 x 200g pouch of Chestnut Purée
- 150g dark chocolate (with a minimum 70% cocoa solids)
- 300ml double cream
- 3 tbsp milk

Optional toppings
- whipped cream
- chocolate shavings
- chopped nuts

METHOD

1. In a large bowl or a stand mixer, whisk together the egg yolks, sugar and chestnut purée for 5 minutes or until the mixture is fluffy and doubled in size.

2. Finely chop the chocolate.

3. Heat the cream and milk until boiling. Take the pan off the heat and whisk in the chopped chocolate until smooth. Pour onto the egg mixture, whisking constantly until almost cool.

4. Divide the mixture between small serving dishes – we like to use pretty glasses – and leave to set in the fridge for at least 2 hours or overnight.

5. Serve the chocolate pots plain or top with spoonfuls of whipped cream, the chocolate shavings and chopped nuts.

LENTIL & RICE CRÊPES WITH MANGO, LIME & COCONUT

The inspiration for these comes from the crispy lentil and rice dosas made in southern India. These ones are easy to prepare and are gluten and dairy-free as well as vegan. To make them savoury, replace the vanilla and sugar with spices.

 MAKES 4   4.5 HRS   VEGAN

INGREDIENTS
- 150g dried Puy Lentils
- 100g white long grain or basmati rice
- 2 tsp sugar
- ½ tsp vanilla paste or 1 tsp vanilla extract
- 1 tsp coconut oil

To serve
- 1 mango
- finely grated zest and juice of 1 lime
- 2 tbsp dairy-free coconut yoghurt
- 2 tbsp toasted coconut flakes
- fresh mint leaves
- maple or agave syrup

METHOD
1. Rinse the lentils and rice in separate sieves by running cold water over them and tip into separate bowls.

2. Blend the lentils and rice separately in a food processor, each with 1 teaspoon of sugar, to a fine powder and return to their bowls. Add 150ml water to each bowl so the powders are just covered and leave in a warm place overnight with a plate or non-airtight lid on top so each can ferment slowly.

3. After soaking and fermenting, each mixture should look a little bubbly. Mix both together and them blend them with the vanilla.

4. Place a crêpe pan over a high heat and add the coconut oil. Wipe out the pan with kitchen paper and spoon in a ladleful of batter. Swirl the pan so the batter coats the base in a thin, even layer. Cook the crêpe until the edges start to turn golden, flip it over and cook the other side for 2 minutes. Slide the crêpe out of the pan onto a plate and keep warm while you cook the remaining mixture to make 4 crêpes.

5. To serve, peel the mango and slice the flesh away from the stone. Divide the crêpes and mango slices between serving plates. Squeeze over the lime juice and top with the yoghurt, toasted coconut flakes, lime zest, some mint leaves, and a drizzle of maple or agave syrup.

If you prefer, you can cook the crêpes after the lentils and rice have been soaking for only 4 hours. However, the crêpes will have a more interesting flavour if they ferment slowly by being soaked overnight. This will also help the body break down the starch more easily.

RASPBERRY & LEMON CHEESECAKE WITH A SUPER SEED CRUST

Cheesecakes will always be popular, whatever the ages of the friends and family members you're feeding, and this recipe is no exception. The super seed and oat base is flavoured with tangy lemon and warm ginger and the rich, cream cheese filling is topped with fresh raspberries.

 SERVES 8   3 HRS   VEGETARIAN

INGREDIENTS

For the base
- 50g butter, plus extra for greasing
- 1 x 250g pouch of ready cooked Super Seeds with Quinoa & Chia
- 100g rolled oats
- finely grated zest of ½ lemon
- 1 tsp ground ginger

For the filling
- 100g raspberries
- 190g icing sugar, sifted
- 2 x 280g packs of full-fat soft cream cheese
- 1 tsp vanilla paste or 2 tsp vanilla extract
- finely grated zest and juice of ½ lemon
- 150ml double cream

To decorate
- 200g raspberries
- finely grated lemon zest

METHOD

1. Preheat the oven to 200°C (180°C fan)/Gas mark 6.

2. Grease and line the base of a 23-cm springform tin with a circle of greaseproof paper and the sides of the tin with a strip.

3. Melt the butter in a small pan. Put the seeds, oats, lemon zest and ground ginger in a food processor and reduce to crumbs. With the motor running, pour the melted butter down the feeder tube and process until you have a crumbly mix. Tip into the tin and press the crumbs over the base and up the sides in an even layer. Make sure the crumbs are pressed down firmly so they don't collapse. Bake in the oven for 20–25 minutes until golden. Leave to cool in the tin.

4. To make the filling, crush the raspberries with 40g of the icing sugar in a bowl. Beat together the cream cheese, vanilla, remaining 150g icing sugar, and lemon zest and juice in a large mixing bowl or stand mixer until smooth. Gradually pour in the cream, continuing to whisk on slow speed until it is incorporated. Take care not to over whisk or the filling will have a grainy appearance.

5. Making sure the base is completely cold, layer the cream cheese mixture and crushed raspberries on top and swirl with a skewer to marble the two together.

6. Decorate the top of the cheesecake with raspberries and a sprinkling of finely grated lemon zest. Chill for at least 2 hours before serving.

RHUBARB, QUINOA & HONEY PUDDING

This lovely cake has a sticky rhubarb and orange topping. Eat it on its own with a cup of tea, or serve it as a dessert, topped with warm custard or tangy crème fraîche.

 SERVES 4-6   50 MINS   Ⓥ VEGETARIAN

INGREDIENTS

- 1 x 250g pouch of ready cooked Red & White Quinoa
- 125g butter, diced and softened, plus extra for greasing
- 75g caster sugar
- 2 large free-range eggs
- 125g self-raising flour
- 1 tsp baking powder
- 5 tbsp runny honey
- 300–400g rhubarb, leaves discarded and stalks chopped into 5cm lengths
- juice of 1 orange
- 1 tbsp demerara sugar

METHOD

1. Preheat the oven to 200°C (180°C fan)/Gas mark 6.

2. Grease a deep, 19cm round cake tin and line with baking parchment.

3. Spread the quinoa out on a baking sheet and dry it out in the oven for 15 minutes. Transfer to a plate and leave to cool.

4. Using an electric hand whisk, cream the butter and sugar together until light and fluffy. Beat in the eggs, one at a time, until mixed in. Sift in the flour and baking powder and gradually stir in with the honey. Stir in all the quinoa and half the rhubarb, reserving the rest for the topping.

5. Spoon the mixture into the cake tin and smooth level. Press the remaining rhubarb on top and pour over the orange juice. Sprinkle the demerara sugar over.

6. Bake for 30–35 minutes or until the point of a knife or a skewer pushed into the centre of the cake comes out clean. Leave to cool in the tin for 10 minutes before turning out and removing the lining paper. Serve the cake warm on its own with tea or coffee, or as a dessert with custard and extra stewed rhubarb if you like.

BANANA, FREEKEH & CARAMEL CAKE

We like to serve this cake while it is still warm, accompanied with caramel sauce. However, once cold, the cake will easily keep for a week in an airtight container or it can be frozen. The roasted freekeh adds a chewy texture and lovely nutty flavour.

 SERVES 12–15   1 HR 10 MINS   VEGETARIAN

INGREDIENTS

For the cake
- 180g soft brown sugar
- 80g dark muscovado sugar, plus an extra 20g for the topping
- 150g butter, melted and cooled, plus extra for greasing
- 200g mashed banana (about 2 bananas), plus 2 small bananas, peeled and halved lengthways, for the top of the cake
- 2 free-range eggs
- 1 tsp baking powder
- 1 tsp bicarbonate of soda
- 375g plain flour
- 1 x 250g pouch of ready cooked Freekeh

For the caramel sauce
- 100g dark muscovado sugar
- 30g butter
- 300ml double cream

METHOD

1. To make the cake, preheat the oven to 200°C (180°C fan)/ Gas mark 6. Grease a 23cm square baking tin and line with baking parchment.

2. Put the soft brown and muscovado sugars in a mixing bowl or the bowl of a stand mixer and whisk in the melted butter for about 3 minutes.

3. Add the mashed banana and whisk until smooth. Beat in the eggs, one at a time, until evenly combined.

4. Sift in the baking powder, bicarbonate of soda and flour, add the freekeh, and fold everything in until incorporated.

5. Spoon the mixture into the prepared baking tin. It should be about half full, as the cake will rise a lot in the oven.

6. Bake for 25 minutes. Remove from the oven and carefully place the banana halves on top. Sprinkle over the 20g muscovado sugar and immediately return the cake to the oven. Bake for a further 25–30 minutes or until the point of a knife comes out clean when pushed into the centre of the cake.

7. While the cake is baking, make the caramel sauce. Heat the sugar and butter in a small saucepan over a medium heat. When the sugar starts to dissolve, add the cream and bring to the boil, stirring constantly until all the sugar has dissolved and you have a thick caramel sauce.

8. Turn out the cake while still warm. Slice and serve with the caramel sauce poured over.

CHOCOLATE, PISTACHIO & CHESTNUT TRUFFLES

These smooth, creamy truffles make the perfect gift, after-dinner treat or light dessert. They can be made ahead of time and frozen before bringing out to defrost 30 minutes before serving.

 MAKES 25-30   1 HR   VEGETARIAN

INGREDIENTS

- 1 x 180g pouch of ready roasted Whole Chestnuts
- 50g pistachios
- 50g hazelnuts
- 200g dark chocolate, chopped
- 100ml double cream

To decorate
- 150g dark chocolate, chopped
- dried edible rose petals
- finely chopped pistachios

METHOD

1. Line a 20cm square baking tin with cling film.

2. Roughly chop the chestnuts, pistachios and hazelnuts in a food processor or with a large knife.

3. Put the chocolate in a heatproof bowl. Heat the cream in a small saucepan until it comes to a simmer, then pour it over the chocolate, stirring constantly until the chocolate has melted and is smooth and glossy.

4. Stir in the chopped nuts and pour into the baking tray. Leave to cool, then chill in the fridge for about 1 hour until just set.

5. Roll the mixture into walnut-size balls or cut the block into squares – whichever you prefer.

6. To decorate the truffles, melt the chocolate in a heatproof bowl over a pan of simmering water or on the defrost setting in the microwave. Using a fork, dip each truffle in the chocolate until coated, shaking off any excess and letting it drip back into the bowl. Place the truffles on a rack over a sheet of baking parchment to catch any further drips.

7. Decorate with rose petals and pistachios while the chocolate is still soft. Store in the fridge or freezer until needed, but remember to remove the truffles from the freezer 30 minutes before serving.

CHOCOLATE & CHESTNUT RIPPLE ICE CREAM

This dark chocolate ice cream, rippled with chestnut and vanilla, is totally irresistible! It is made by combining two different ice cream recipes but if you prefer, you could just make one or the other.

 MAKES 2 LITRES   2.5 HRS   (V) VEGETARIAN

INGREDIENTS

For the base for both ice creams
- 10 free-range egg yolks
- 200g caster sugar
- 500ml milk
- 900ml double cream

For the chocolate ice cream
- 75g dark chocolate, finely chopped
- 20g cocoa powder

For the chestnut ice cream
- 1 x 200g pouch of Chestnut Purée
- ½ tsp vanilla paste or 1 tsp vanilla extract

To serve
- chopped roasted chestnuts

METHOD

1. To make the base for both ice creams, in a large mixing bowl and using an electric hand whisk, or in a stand mixer, whisk together the egg yolks and sugar for about 5 minutes until thick and fluffy.

2. Pour the milk and cream into a large saucepan, place over a medium heat and bring to a simmer.

3. While the milk and cream are heating, put the chopped chocolate and cocoa in one large bowl (for the chocolate ice cream), and mix the chestnut purée and vanilla together until smooth in another bowl (for the chestnut ice cream).

4. When the milk and cream are hot, pour about 100ml into each bowl, whisking both to melt the chocolate and the chestnut mixtures.

5. Pour the remaining milk and cream into the egg yolk mixture and whisk for 1 minute. Divide evenly between the chocolate and chestnut bowls, stirring to remove any lumps.

6. Take 2 clean pans and pour a custard into each. Place one pan over a gentle heat and cook for about 3–4 minutes, stirring constantly until the custard is thick enough to coat the back of a spoon, or the temperature reaches 75°C on a cooking thermometer. Pass the custard quickly through a fine sieve into a clean bowl and press a sheet of cling film over the surface to prevent a skin forming. Stand the bowl in a larger bowl containing cold water and ice cubes to cool it down quickly. Repeat with the other pan to make a second custard.

7. Churn the custards separately in an ice cream machine according to the manufacturer's instructions, then ripple them together in a large tray or ice cream tub.

8. Freeze for about 1 hour or until ready to serve. Scoop the ice cream into dishes and sprinkle with roasted chestnuts.

CHOCOLATE SLICE WITH PEANUT BUTTER & JAM

The crunchy super seed and oat flapjack base is first topped with layers of jam and peanut butter and then covered in a thick swirl of white and milk chocolate. Sheer indulgence doesn't even come close to describing this oh-so-tempting teatime treat.

 MAKES 10–12 SLICES 2 HRS VEGETARIAN

INGREDIENTS

- 1 x 250g pouch of ready cooked Super Seeds with Quinoa & Chia
- 80g jumbo rolled oats
- 50g demerara sugar
- 1 free-range egg
- 2 tbsp raspberry or strawberry jam
- 340g jar of peanut butter
- 100g white chocolate, chopped
- 100g milk chocolate, chopped

METHOD

1. Preheat the oven to 200°C (180°C fan)/Gas mark 6. Line a 20-cm square baking tin with baking parchment.

2. Pulse the super seeds, oats, sugar and egg together in a food processor and press the mixture firmly into the base of the tin, smoothing the top with the back of a spoon. Bake for 20 minutes until golden brown.

3. While it is still warm, spread the jam over the flapjack base and leave to cool.

4. Warm the peanut butter in a small pan until easily spreadable. Spread it on top of the jam. Chill in the fridge for about 40 minutes.

5. Melt the chocolates in separate bowls over pans of simmering water, without letting the bottoms of the bowls touch the water, or on the defrost setting in the microwave. Stir the chocolates until smooth and glossy.

6. Drizzle the chocolates alternately over the peanut butter layer and then swirl together to create a marbled effect. Leave in the fridge until set – about 30 minutes.

7. When ready to serve, cut into squares with a hot knife so the chocolate topping doesn't crack and you get nice even squares that show all the tempting layers.

ETON MESS PAVLOVA WITH CHESTNUT & CHERRY CREAM

Like all the best pavlovas, this meringue is crisp on the outside and soft and chewy in the middle. Don't worry if it cracks while it is cooling – homemade pavlovas nearly always do and you can be proud it's all your own work!

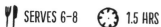 SERVES 6–8   1.5 HRS   (V) VEGETARIAN

INGREDIENTS

For the meringue
- 1 tsp vinegar, plus extra for the bowl
- 6 free-range egg whites
- 300g golden caster sugar
- 1 tsp cornflour

For the chestnut & cherry cream
- 300ml double cream
- 80g icing sugar
- 1 x 200g pouch of Chestnut Purée
- 1 x 400g can of black cherries in light syrup

To serve
- 1 x 180g pouch of ready roasted Whole Chestnuts
- 200g fresh cherries

METHOD

1. Preheat the oven to 170°C (150°C fan)/Gas mark 3.

2. To make the meringue, using a sheet of kitchen paper towel, wipe the inside of a large mixing bowl with vinegar. Add the egg whites and whisk until they are standing in firm peaks. Gradually whisk in the sugar, a little at a time, until it has all been added. Whisk in the cornflour and vinegar – this will help stabilize the meringue – and continue whisking for about another 5 minutes until the whites are stiff and shiny.

3. Draw a circle roughly the size of a dinner plate on a sheet of baking parchment and place it upside down on a baking sheet, dabbing a little meringue on the underside to keep the parchment in place. Spoon the meringue onto the circle to fill it with billowy clouds that have lots of texture. Save 3–4 generous tablespoons to pipe tubes or other smaller shapes onto a second baking sheet lined with baking parchment. Or, simply spread this meringue onto the parchment so it can be broken up and used to fill the finished dessert.

4. Bake the meringues in the oven for 10 minutes, then lower the temperature to 130°C (110°C fan)/Gas mark 1 and bake for 1 hour. Turn off the oven and leave the meringues to cool inside. When cold, remove them from the parchment.

5. To make the chestnut & cherry cream, whisk the cream with the sugar until soft peaks form. Fold in the chestnut purée. Drain and pit the cherries, reserving the syrup from the can, and fold the cherries into the cream.

6. To assemble, chop the cooked chestnuts into chunks. Pile the chestnut and cherry cream and meringue pieces onto the pavlova base and decorate with the chestnuts and fresh cherries. Drizzle over some syrup from the can of cherries.

INDEX

158